Big, Bold and Beautiful

Big, Bold and Beautiful

Living large on a small planet

Jackqueline Hope

Macmillan Canada
Toronto

Canadian Cataloguing in Publication Data

Hope, Jackqueline, 1956–
    Big, bold and beautiful : living large on a small planet

ISBN 0-7715-7381-2

1. Hope, Jackqueline, 1956–   2. Self-acceptance.
3. Obesity – Psychological aspects.   4. Overweight
women – Mental health.   5. Overweight women –
Canada – Biography.   I. Title.

RC552. 025H66   1996   362.1'96398' 0092   C96–930063–8

Macmillan Canada wishes to thank the Canada Council, the Ontario Arts Council
and the Ontario Ministry of Culture and Communications for supporting its
publishing program.

Cover design: Gillian Tsintziras/The Brookview Group
Cover photographs: Dan Couto
Hair and make-up: Paul Langill

Macmillan Canada
A Division of Canada Publishing Corporation

Toronto, Canada

1 2 3 4 5   00 99 98 97 96
Printed in Canada

For Darlene

ACKNOWLEDGMENTS

There are many people who influence a life. I'd like to thank those who made my story come together.

Philip, you are and always have been my purpose, my meaning, and my will to continue. I'm so proud of the fine, young man you've become. Keep strong, and keep growing in mind and spirit. I love you, my son.

Mom and Dad, I deeply love both of you. Thank you for giving me morals, scruples and respect. All these qualities have built my foundation of hope. Without your support and love, it would not have been possible.

A personal thank you to all of my family and good friends for your unflagging love, encouragement and understanding. You've put up with unreturned phone calls and my bowing out of many social gatherings. For this, I owe you. (Candy, thank you, you make me laugh — you make me laugh.)

Rebecca, I miss you.

To all of my wonderful Big, Bold & Beautiful staff: I've been absent for the past year, on and off, and I realize you guys worked your tushes off to maintain the high standards of our company. Thanks for putting up with my moods, bringing me pots of tea, and listening with enthusiasm as I read you chapter after chapter. Love you guys.

Thanks, coach, for believing in me, for keeping me focused and motivated, and for teaching me how to sweat and feel terrific doing it. Thanks for never giving up. I love you, Keith, and I'm deeply grateful.

I'm obliged to all of my Plus-Figure Models who continue to carry on my legacy.

I appreciate all of the clients, photographers, and make-up and hair stylists who have supported me in the past and continue to do so. Kudos to Barbara Alexander, who never had to be reminded that big was beautiful, who always put my best face forward, and who never gave me a chignon. Love ya.

And I must acknowledge the large-size designers and manufacturers who have put up with my complaints and grown with me.

Countless newspapers, television and radio talk shows deserve tremendous applause and heartfelt gratitude for allowing me to bring forth my vision and philosophy over the years. Thanks for spreading our message that beauty does not stop at size 8.

A hand also goes to all big, bold and beautiful people around the globe who have joined me in the celebration of size acceptance.

I'm also indebted to the folks who helped make the book come together, those who shared their thoughts and beliefs with me: Gail Marchessault, Dr. Manly Spigelman, Eleanor Brownridge, Dr. Linda McCargar, Sylvie Patry and Andria Siegler.

Thank you to all the big shots. Your words are more powerful than you can imagine, and they strongly reinforced everything I stood for over the years: Size is never an issue.

Trisse, thank you for listening to my every beat and for being there to wipe my tears. You have been an incredibly supportive collaborator and comrade. The past year, you graciously put your size 8 body aside and enthusiastically stepped into my large world. For this, I love you, Bamboo, and I respect you very much.

Jane, your guidance and encouragement provided me with many insights. Without you, this book would still be in my head. Thanks, doll, you're the greatest.

And I owe much to my editor, Nicole, whose thoughtful encouragement, keen persistence and belief in my beliefs made this book possible.

And, finally, Peter, my love. From day one, you've been my guiding light and my knight in shining armour. You've allowed me to believe in fairy tales and encouraged me to reach for my dreams. You made it possible for me to step into the limelight, and you've lovingly guided me through every hill and valley. You pulled me up when I was down, made me smile when I was crying, you were my compass when I was lost, and you led me on a journey that would have made Cinderella envious. Please don't pinch me, for if I'm dreaming I don't ever want to wake up.

Preface

When she was fourteen, a modelling agency said her face was too fat. It was a death sentence. Sheena Carpenter died in November 1993. She was found on the kitchen floor of her apartment by her mother. She weighed 50 pounds. She was twenty-two. The answer to why Sheena died is complex. But it probably can be found somewhere in the intricate intermix of the beauty myth, with an unfathomable, unreasonable quest for physical perfection and relentless social pressure.

—from the mission statement of Sheena's Place, a
non-profit organization devoted to the treatment and
support of those suffering eating disorders.

Not surprisingly, today's media pander to public fear, rather than educate their readers or reshape public opinion. Women's magazines, for more than half a century, have exploited the fear of fat. Promoting discontent and selling false hopes, they have enslaved women of all ages to endless variations of diet and exercise regimes, guaranteeing the ideal body.

An average North-American high-fashion model is 5'10", 115 pounds, compared to the average North American woman, who stands 5'4" and weighs 145 pounds. Look at the slick, glossy fashion magazines. At the moment, model Kate Moss is the epitome of ideal. Considered beautiful, she's 5'8" and appears prepubescent.

Her colleagues are similiar—visible ribs, no breasts. When is enough enough?

Big, Bold and Beautiful grapples with this unseemly preoccupation. I, like most women—women of all ages, shapes and weight—have lived this struggle. My story, your story, is one and the same.

In my life, I have overcome a period of depression, self-hatred and feelings of worthlessness. I allowed other people to control my life. It was only when I developed the courage and the strength to fight back was I able to win my inner battle.

On these pages there is a method to the madness. My story of how to live large on a small planet. It's written so that you can take my hand, engage your heart, and journey to the land of the guilt-free.

This story may sound very familiar, but it's meant to. There are things we need to relive—valuable things we need so desperately to remind ourselves of—that make the journey easier. They are the things that make it possible to live your life to the fullest and, hopefully, never look back along the path.

I would be honoured if my story spared just one person a single tear, and I would be more than blessed if I could change a life.

CONTENTS

The Big Picture

WE LIVE IN A TIME and place where thin is in. This, of course, is not news to any of us. However, it is new. When you look back through the records of human history, you'll find our current ideal of thinness is not only unconventional, it's downright unnatural. In fact, you'll find plump was positively perfect in the past.

In his book *The Body Reader: Social Aspects of the Human Body*, anthropologist Ted Polhemus writes, "it is necessary to pause and remind ourselves that in other societies and historical periods girls who looked like Twiggy would have had to resign themselves either to camouflage or to staying at home."

It's true. One of the oldest artifacts still remaining from prehistoric time is a sculpture so small it most likely would fit in your hand. It may be small, but in no way is it tiny. It's called the Venus of Willendorf, and it's a her. This small sculpture is of a very well-rounded woman—her breasts are more than ample, her belly is rotund, her hips are wide and full. She may or may not have been an idol; what's certain is she was ideal.

Back in 10,000 B.C., bulging buttocks, wide thighs, thick arms and bellies were sexy. So much so, both men and women tied tight bands or belts just above areas they wanted to accentuate to induce extra bulging.

Through the centuries that followed, an abundance of flesh competed against other silhouettes for top billing, but more often than not extra flesh won out.

In medieval times, Queen Isabella, a woman of substance herself, made round figures fashionable. During her reign, as well as after, women unfortunate enough to be thin tied pillows around their stomachs and hid them beneath their dresses.

Plumpness simply grew in popularity. Renaissance men stuffed the fronts of their shirts to create great pot bellies, while women wore birdcage-like contraptions, called farthingales, under their skirts to produce hips at least two feet across.

By the time Queen Victoria settled her majestic bottom into the British throne, being large was a luxury. It meant you could afford the brandy, the tea cakes and the goose-liver pâté; if you were a woman, it also meant you had the physical strength to carry your clothes, which during this period weighed more than ten pounds.

Throughout history, Western culture was not alone in its fondness for fat. Other cultures also held the belief, and many continue to do so.

The Tuareg tribe of the Sahara believe beauty equals big—beautiful women crawl because their legs are no longer strong enough to hold their bodies erect. In certain areas of West Africa, young women are sent to "fattening houses," where they are fed balls of bread (sometimes for as long as a year) so they emerge plump enough to interest worthy suitors. In fact, at present there are at least a dozen different tribes and cultures around the globe that believe big is best.

However, in our society body sizes stopped happily bouncing along in the '20s, when flappers began wrapping their bosoms and hips for a more boyish effect. After that, all hell broke loose.

Ever so slowly, but equally as surely, the ideal female body began to lose weight. And, just to confirm to Western culture that there was in fact an "ideal," the American Metropolitan Life Insurance Company invented something called an ideal weight chart.

If you were a woman in 1959, for example, and you happened to stand 5' 6", ideally you would weigh anywhere from 114 to 146 pounds, to be exact (and they were). Surprisingly, thirty years later ideal body weights grew; not surprisingly, they didn't grow by much. If you happened to be a 5' 6" female in 1989, the scale would ideally point between 120 and 159. (No doubt, Queen Victoria would not have been amused.)

Cultural anthropologists, historians, feminists and sociologists all find various meanings and culprits in the thinning trend; some agree, some don't. But there is one simple underlying fact that seems to make sense: men are judged on how they perform; girls and women are judged on how they look. Of course it's nonsensical, nonetheless in our society it's true.

Dr. Manly Spigelman, University of Winnipeg professor of psychology (who also acted as advisor on the Canadian film *Fat Chance*) also finds it nonsensical. In fact, he finds a lot of things nonsensical.

As he sees it, "The '60s established an anorexic ideal. With Twiggy, women strived for thinness, and starving became an ideal. In the '70s, we had Jane Fonda—now you had to be thin and fit. And as if that wasn't enough aggravation, the '80s brought a need to wear padded shoulders, to have 'power lunches,' and be successful. In the '90s, you have to have all these things, plus you have to look like you work out with weights—basically, you have to look like an athlete."

His reason for why this is happening is just as simple. "We no longer live in a society that reveres spiritual or intellectual achievement. All we have left is a body. We use our bodies as a metaphor for identity. And, if you don't eat in the correct way, exercise in the correct way, or look the correct way, you're devalued. It's a sad time we're living in. It's a dreadful time to be physically deviant and held responsible."

The fact is, we're held responsible for something over which we have no control. Women are naturally fatter than men—a healthy young woman is 24 percent body fat; a healthy young man is 16 percent body fat. As Spigelman says, "Evolution made women fat."

And, to him, this is the maddening part. "I am not penalized for being shorter—in our society we would view that as absurd and evil. However, when it comes to fatness, somehow society seems to think it's okay to stigmatize. Larger people are held responsible for something they can neither hide nor control. It's a myth that you can do something about it. Diet pills and all those weight-loss methods fail—they all fail."

They may fail, but that doesn't stop the ideal, nor does it stop people from trying to attain it.

In 1993, Gail Marchessault, dietitian and nutritionist, conducted a study at the University of Manitoba to research body images and ideals of thirteen-year-old girls as well as their mothers. She discovered a variety of facts, but at the bottom of it all she found "the way they talked about weight presented a coherent pattern of society in which concern about weight is a normal reaction."

She noticed "girls and women talked about being looked at and judged—never in an appreciative way; always in a negative way.... Everyone said appearance was not a good way to choose your friends; although they thought that was how others chose them. They talked about not judging other people, or judging others on their weight, but had difficulty not judging themselves that way."

It's obvious many of us judge ourselves against an ideal. But, unfortunately, we seem to have forgotten what the word means. If you look it up in the dictionary, you find "a concept of perfection," "a high principle; lofty aim," and "that which exists only as a concept of the mind." It was something Marchessault realized many of her study's participants overlooked: "They didn't seem to understand that ideal wasn't attainable."

ONE

In Search of the Perfect Body

THE TURNING POINT in my life that started the questioning of my body happened well after puberty. From the time I was small to the age of fifteen, I didn't think much about my body. It just carried me through and functioned well. Boys were attracted to it. I felt sexy at times. Sometimes I didn't feel so great. But my feelings about the size of my body never came up. They weren't a concern.

At fifteen, I wore a size 10 and was about 130 pounds. I wasn't worried about my weight, but I was still trying to conform to the idea that I had to be perfect. Although it had nothing to do with my size, I was still trying to change what I had to make me look better. Even at that tender age I was thinking, "if only I had..."

My nose was one example. I thought I had a very long nose, like my father, and I was afraid it was going to get even longer (maybe because I told so many little, white lies). I was always trying to shove my nose back.

I would sit in the classroom and actually try to push it back with my hand. Of course, it didn't work; however, today I have a bump on my nose to show for my efforts. What I wanted was a cute, little, pudgy nose. Never got it.

I also put two-sided tape behind my ears. I hated the way they looked. They stuck out. I never even thought of pulling my hair back into a ponytail, for fear someone would call me Dumbo. (It was a whole other revelation when they started calling me Dumbo for my size—they never once mentioned or noticed my ears.)

On special occasions, I'd also stuff my bra with tissue. Lots of other girls were doing it—I desired that buxom look and thought it was a trendy thing to do.

So there I was with what I thought was a long nose (no doubt red from all that shoving), my taped-back ears and Kleenex in my bra. I was a real sight to behold. I didn't feel comfortable at the age of fifteen, but I certainly wasn't worried about the size or the contours of my body. I didn't pay much attention to it; it was fine the way it was.

However, that all changed just a few, short years later. At the age of eighteen, I was about to marry my first husband, Gus, and I was about to go shopping for my first wedding dress.

I grew up in the small, northern Canadian town of Huntsville, Ontario, where there were no wedding gowns for sale. For that, we had to travel one hundred miles south to a small city, Barrie. This trip was a very significant part of my life, because it was the first time I realized there was another world besides the one in which I lived. To my surprise, there was a place beyond our small-town borders where pain was inflicted on people who were larger than a size 12.

Before the expedition, I consumed every bridal magazine I could lay my hands on. Prior to this, I really hadn't read many fashion magazines — first of all, I couldn't really afford them; secondly, I was busy working from the age of fourteen and there was no time to leaf. But for my wedding day, I wanted to be prepared. I wanted to know what was available, and I wanted to figure out what I wanted.

I wanted a lot. It was 1974, and the bridal magazines were full of thin, snub-nosed, blonde brides with their perfect bodies, impeccable skin and elaborate wedding gowns. I spent hours gazing at them.

The shopping trip, to my disappointment, was no comparison. First I found that I was not a size 12. Although I was a size 12 in regular clothing, bridal wear is made two sizes smaller. I was suddenly a size 16. This led to the second realization. Our long journey to this small city still left me with very little selection.

I remember trying on the wedding dress — the one token dress they had that was closest to my size. It had a high collar up to the chin and a big bow on the behind.

I remember going to the tiny change room with my fingers crossed and my eyes lowered, praying that one-and-only dress would fit. I knew if it fit, or almost fit, my mom would buy it. It almost fit.

On the way home with my package, my mom made it impossible to overlook the fact that I was a little too big. In her eyes, I was suddenly overweight. She suggested I go on a diet. I was stunned.

This dress, my fantasy dress, was no longer a dream; it had become a living, breathing and horribly threatening challenge. It was my first introduction to the diet world of hell.

Yes, the dress was too tight. And yes, my parents bought it for me on their modest income. It had to fit, and the only way I knew it would was if I lost at least twenty pounds—an entire dress size.

All the way home, I kept thinking about it. I'd never been on a diet. I didn't know how to accomplish it. It was so foreign.

I realized I was being forced into this situation for the simple and ridiculous reason that the fashion industry was too stupid to recognize there were people like me who couldn't find a wedding dress in a bigger size. How ironic—I was more of a person, but I was being made to feel like less of one.

Nonetheless, this anger lasted all of a few seconds. Fear took over. "What is this?" I wondered. "What is a diet? I love the way I am. Why do I have to lower myself to this?"

But I knew the answer. I had to fit into that miserable dress. The wedding suddenly seemed like a curse. I hated that dress from day one—even before I got married.

That shopping incident proved to me I was bigger than average, and overnight I became painfully self-conscious about my body. It's hard to feel good about yourself when the availability of wedding gowns disappears because of your size.

However, when I gazed in the mirror, I still liked what I saw, and this became unbearably confusing. I began to question myself. I began to wonder if I was different, and why. I still liked who I was, but I knew it was going to be difficult being the size I was.

The next shock to my system happened a few months later, when I was trying on swimsuits for my honeymoon. I was exceptionally critical of my size. I'd had the time to scrutinize my body and find out precisely what was wrong. All I could find wrong was a bulge on each side of my inner thigh. And this was where I rested my decision to buy a bathing suit. Of course, there wasn't a bathing suit made that hid the upper thigh, so I decided against it altogether.

Before, I'd actually felt quite beautiful in a bikini, but I was afraid other people, including my soon-to-be husband, would see the fat on my upper thighs. I couldn't allow that to happen. So, instead, I spent my honeymoon on a South Carolina beach in a halter top and hot pants that hid my thigh bulge.

I had never looked to see how big my body was or wasn't until that experience with the wedding dress. Being the second youngest in a family of five children, I wore a lot of hand-me-downs — my brothers' sweaters, my sisters' cast-offs. I wore uniforms to school, and when I got a part-time job at a hotel, I had a uniform there as well. Whenever I did shop, and I loved clothes, I don't remember having a problem finding things that fit.

But after my wedding day, I started going into stores to observe the choices available to me. More often than not, I noticed stores offered flowered, shapeless caftans and ugly, polyester pants in my size range. It really frightened me. I started to look at myself through the availability of clothing, and how others were seeing me. If it was normal to be the way I was, why was it impossible to dress fashionably at this size?

Oddly enough, it was only a few years before this that I'd worn a bikini, feeling really good about myself. I stood proudly while a photographer from the local newspaper took pictures. I never thought about my size; I thought he wanted to take my photo because I looked good. In fact, I had modelled a few times in my late

teens. I posed for a Holiday Inn brochure, grand open-
ings of car dealerships and vacation travel guides. I was
not inhibited, nor was I vain, about my body. It was just
my body.

No doubt, this earlier experience of accepting my
body only added to the crushing realization that I was
different. I felt different.

On my honeymoon, my husband Gus couldn't help
but notice I wasn't wearing a bathing suit on the beach,
and he asked why. I simply told him I couldn't find one.
So he took me out to look for one. In the middle of
South Carolina, in the middle of a store packed with racks
of swimwear in every imaginable size, I could hardly use
the excuse of not being able to find one. I had to give
him some reason. I told him what I thought was the
truth; I told him I was too fat for a bathing suit and was
embarrassed to wear one.

After my son Philip was born, a year later, my hand-
me-downs weren't fitting. My maternity clothes were
ragged and tight. I spent hours scouring the shops looking for one more baggy, one-size-fits-all frock, but to my
dismay, they simply didn't have clothing to fit my body.
At this point, I became very susceptible to criticism,
especially my husband's, and even more confused.

Why was my husband becoming so cruel? Why was he
making such insulting comments about my size? Why
couldn't I find anything that fit? I kept asking myself
these questions over and over.

I stood in front of the mirror, trying to find ways of
appreciating my body, trying to teach myself and talk
myself into loving it. I wasn't going to hate it just because
it didn't fit into a wedding dress, nor was I going to hate
it because others were finding it unattractive.

Those who once accepted me were now saying, "You were such a pretty girl. Remember when you used to model? You used to have such a terrific body."

The self-hatred was twice as available as it had been on the day I looked for a wedding dress. My body proportions dramatically changed after my son was born. If I wanted, there was now an abundance of opinions and beliefs I could latch onto.

Although when I looked in the mirror I knew who I was, the person staring back was constantly changing. Now I needed even more control of my feelings. I needed to be more in control of who I was, because I was constantly trying to confirm that I was still okay.

After a while, I really had no idea who I was, except for the part of me that could be defined by measurements, scales, clothing and rude, insulting remarks.

I would look hard in the mirror. I'd study my face. This segment of my body was very familiar to me. They say the eyes are a mirror of the soul, and I would look to see if I could glean some hint of the spirit within. The harder I looked, the more I realized my face was a legacy of those who had gone before me — my grandmother's jawline, my grandfather's droopy eyelid, my mother's smile, my father's nose. In this ancestral mask I felt sudden pride.

My broad shoulders came alive with strength and character. I noticed my arms were strong, but gentle. I cradled my newborn sweetness in those arms. I put them around people I loved. They lugged groceries, laundry and garbage, and I'd always taken them for granted. I held myself with them, wrapped those long arms around me and gave myself a hug.

My breasts had always been a source of pride and pleasure for me, and with the additional weight they were even fuller and more ample, proportional to my heavier hips. My belly, with its marks of childbearing, was cause for celebration, as it was this part of my body that truly nurtured my little miracle of life. My strong legs held me up, and through thick and thin they never failed me.

My refound joy in my body caused a leak in the dyke of my confusion. I moved my hands over my full body and caressed the softness of myself every day. I closed off the judgements of others, and in my mind I became that innocent, young girl again. I rekindled the rich feeling of freedom that says, "I love myself the way I am, for I am beautiful."

It was a thought and belief I never let go. Sometimes it was camouflaged or ignored, but the belief never left. I was able to recapture it when I stopped allowing others to think and believe for me.

From then on, the mirror was very close to me. I didn't hesitate to look back at the reflection. At times I felt alone by looking at my reflection; alone in my feelings. But I knew if I let go of loving myself, I would let go of me. I understood that my body had grown bigger, much bigger, but every part of it had been good to me. That gave me a sense of pride, and a reason to keep on believing.

The only sense of loathing I felt was through others. I liked myself, but I couldn't understand why others didn't. With the insults, the cruel remarks, the suggestions for change, and the eventual abuse from my first husband, I wondered why I liked myself, but it didn't stop me.

There were many times I honestly thought something was wrong with me. I couldn't understand why I liked myself, when the whole world—including the medical profession and my dearest friends and family—was saying something was wrong.

I almost turned my back on that mirror. God knows I tried. I turned my back on my feelings and tried to succumb to others' ideas of perfection. I tried to submit to what everyone else was telling me, because I thought something was unnatural about liking the way I was. But, no matter what, I never disliked my body at any age or any size.

There is a basic fear of abundance in our puritanical society. Fat people personify that fear. We're told we're not powerful, we're not beautiful, we're not healthy, we're not mobile, we're not sexy, and we have no right to take up so much space. I find it a challenge and an amusement to break these so-called rules. In fact, I make it my duty.

As long as I am healthy and active, who cares if I never make the swimsuit issue of *Sports Illustrated*? I admire the woman who feels free to dance naked in the garden no matter what her size.

Big shapes and sizes have their own strength. For a very long time, I've collected Botero paintings. His women are very large, particularly through the hips, thighs and buttocks. They're powerful, energetic, sexy and happy; they're uninhibited. And they're usually pictured in motion—swimming, dancing and, heart be still, eating.

A large person making a powerful move makes fat fascinating. I've always found bigger things playful and seductive somehow. There's a mystical quality to being larger. There's care and compassion in large things. Maybe others view them as insufficient and unnecessary, but I've always viewed them as wanted and cared for. They're huggable and lovable, and for some reason I've never looked at largeness as being wrong. So how could I possibly look in the mirror and think it was wrong? But, unfortunately, life didn't revolve entirely around the mirror.

There was constant brainwashing from the world around me. I heard them out. I listened to their rules. And I tried anything that not only might make them happy, but anything that might prove I was wrong. And, so, I went on a journey.

My journey was to see if they were right. It sounds simple, but it wasn't as simple as that. In a perfect world it would have been very simple. But this journey had a lot of pitfalls; it was a very bumpy road. It wasn't an easy road to follow, but I took it to find out.

Eventually, I came back to where I started. I realized I had liked the original path I'd been going down. It was my path. It was my road to happiness and success, not someone else's.

We all have different paths. We're all from different molds; we're built in different ways with different personalities. Why can't we all have different body sizes? It's a good question, but I travelled down the wrong path for a long time before I came up with an answer.

I didn't really get a good glimpse of society's image of beauty until I moved to the city. When I saw the image of thinness, I thought it was just a personal preference, not a cultural one. I came from a very large family: some were large, some were small. I didn't look at certain body shapes as wrong, merely different. Everybody is different.

It wasn't long after our son was born that Gus and I decided to move south to Toronto. In the city, I found plus-size shops galore. I found wonderful clothing — well, maybe not really wonderful, but there were many things that actually fit.

This was a new revelation of body size. I wasn't the biggest. I developed a different frame of mind when I realized I hadn't reached my limit. There was life after size 22. It was another world; not the world of sizes 4 to 10, but a realm of sizes 12 to 26. It was an environment I could fit into.

Even though I found clothes that fit, it didn't stop the dieting. I was still trying to conform to the wishes of others, mostly those of my first husband. I tried everything I could to grant his wishes, and although I carried a lot of weight, I held no magical powers.

After my first marriage ended, and by the time I reached the age of twenty-four, I came across another revelation. I met my second husband, Peter.

Peter made me feel beautiful from the very beginning. He said he saw something special. He told me I had a certain walk, a certain pride; I had something special that he had never seen before.

Peter and I were very good friends for years. I hadn't a clue he was falling in love with me. I not only didn't expect it, I didn't think I deserved it. During that time, I was separated from my first husband and feeling the damaging effects of that marriage. Peter listened to me — my insecurities, my difficulties, my fears. We were very close. He believed in me completely. He never once talked about my size, we just talked about each other's feelings. There were times I gained weight, times I lost it, but wherever my body took me, it was never an issue with Peter.

The only suggestions he ever made were for my entertainment or well-being—"Let's go for a walk," "Let's see a movie," "Let's do something together." He cared for me and he believed in me. So much so, he introduced me to his agent (Peter was one of Canada's top male models), who took me on as a plus-size model.

Because my family had tried to get me to lose weight, because my first husband had tried to force me to lose weight, and because I had heard the snickering and laughing of children when I walked my son to school, I'd suffered years of guilt. I used to think my body was a shame for others to see (although I didn't find it shameful).

It was mind-boggling when I met Peter. It was strange not to feel guilty or big. I didn't feel any size, I just felt very beautiful. He didn't make me feel small, big or tall. And it was the first confirmation that I wasn't insane. It affirmed that what I saw in the mirror was fine. I was beautiful and I was okay. I knew then there was hope.

There's a wonderful, warm sense of pleasure in knowing you're right. It was a breath of fresh air. It was as if I had finally been let out of prison—the cell doors flew open and I ran, yelling, "Yes, I'm free. Free to believe in something I've always believed in. I'm free to be alive again. I'm free to be who I always thought I was. I'm free to be me."

I realized there were people out there who didn't inflict their beliefs on anyone else, who didn't force their idealism on others. There was another person who felt it was natural—just as I did—to let someone have their own ideals for themselves.

While in my personal life I was free to believe what I wanted, my professional life was not as liberal. As a model, it was difficult. No matter how hard I tried to show the stylists and photographers I was an individual and a "larger" representative, they always tried to make me look thinner. They never showed me at the size I was, and this played havoc with my inner self. Regardless of where I landed on the dress scale—from sizes 14 to 24—they continually tried to make me look like a size 12 or smaller.

They would dress me in non-patterned outfits or they would omit the belt. Anything they could think of that might hide the truth, they tried. In the beginning, they never included me in bathing suit scenes. Showing too much of my body was a definite no-no. Granted, they wanted to include someone who was larger, but they didn't dare overexpose the issue.

This messed up my head because I was so proud of who I was, and I wanted to show that as an example to the world. However, they weren't interested in that. It didn't matter if I was a person with feelings, beliefs and pride. In their eyes, I was simply a product—and products are inanimate.

I still managed to like my body, even though others now seemed to have control over it. Nonetheless, there were times it felt like an inconvenience. I wished I had a magical switch that could make me all the different sizes they wanted. (No doubt, the same type of magical switch I had wanted for my first husband.)

There were also certain modelling experiences that made me feel insecure about my body. I remember one incident that, at the time, was entirely awful—in retrospect it seems almost funny.

I was hired for a major fashion show. There were to be about fourteen different scenes in this particular show, and because I was the token large-size model, I was in almost every one.

Before the rehearsal, I was at my rack of clothing, as all the other models were, looking through the garments they had laid out for me. I knew beforehand they planned a bathing suit scene, so I looked for, but didn't find, a swimsuit. I breathed a sigh of relief.

During the rehearsal, every model gets into her clothes for each scene and lines up with the others, so the choreographer and stylist can ensure the models and outfits mix and match well.

The bathing suit scene rolled around, and all the six-foot models got into their heels and swimsuits and pranced to the front of the room.

All of a sudden I heard someone yell, "Hope? Where are you?"

I separated the clothes on my rack, poked out my head, and yelled back, "What?"

"How come you're not out here?"

"I don't have a bathing suit."

"Oh yes you do," the assistant shot back. "I just forgot to put it on your rack."

Great. My heart started to pound in my chest. I'd have to go out there, about 5'10" in my heels, and stand next to the 6'1", 6'2", and 6'3" models.

Then I looked down. I'd forgotten my heels. So I was back down to my natural 5'8" frame.

It was just about this time they brought me the bathing suit. It was the most ghastly, ugly size 18 bathing suit I'd ever seen, a horrendous mix of fuchsia, lime green and black. (The lime green was polka dots that ran across a black skirt; the top was fuchsia and had the pointiest torpedo bra ever made.) I kept thinking it must be a joke. It had to be a practical joke.

All the models were already lined up in their heels. I came out in this thing, barefoot. It was horrifying.

One of the other models whispered to me, "I can hear the men panting already."

She meant it as a joke, not an insult. And it was funny. I couldn't help but laugh. The bathing suit was hysterical. To make light of the situation, I put my fingertips on my head and twirled around like a ballerina. Everyone started laughing and the choreographer said, "I don't think so. You can change."

The choreographer agreed it was hideous. The salespeople had hand-picked it to be in the show and she thought, with luck, it might complement the others. It didn't. It was appalling, and so was the whole experience. My body didn't embarrass me, the situation did. That bathing suit ridiculed me.

After that, I did wear bathing suits during my modelling career, but they were beautiful bathing suits, not sight-gags. I felt comfortable showing my body in public. It was necessary that people see the size I was; I was hired because of my size. So, at a certain level, modelling made me feel secure about who I was. It justified my size. It gave me permission to be the size I was, and to show that to the public. I didn't have to make excuses anymore just to make others quiet. The simple fact that I was a model and had a mission to be my size gave everyone permission to accept me. Although it was awfully sad, considering others should have accepted me anyway, it gave them a reason to accept me.

Of course, this security was just "at some level," not all levels. Often, on set, stylists would have to cut open my clothing at the back so they could make it bigger, and hold it together with enormous safety pins or masking tape. Again, I'd question, "Is my body too big for the clothes? Should I have lost a bit of weight?" But then, there were days when the clothes hung off me, and the stylists had to grab the material by the handful and pin it back, saying, "We should have gotten someone bigger. These clothes are just too loose on you." I was always too big or too small. I was never exactly what they wanted.

When I eventually became a modelling agent, I created a plus-size agency primarily as a political movement. But like any other multimillion-dollar industry, plus-size modelling is directed largely by financial concerns. The bottom line is economics, not social change. It was disheartening for me to realize business didn't have a lot to do with social impact.

Agency owners like myself have clearly helped the size-acceptance movement, but, unfortunately, it's still in the name of beauty. We hold our models to standards as narrow as those for thin ones. As a rule, most of our clients want plus-size models who are tall, size 14, white, and under the age of twenty-five—just like their thinner counterparts. The industry really hasn't progressed that far.

Although people will say, "Isn't that wonderful? Haven't we come a long way with size?" the size movement still hasn't done an awful lot for an awful lot of people. There is still a narrow spectrum for everything we do.

For such a long time, I had to educate stylists on all the different sizes. They didn't really understand anything above a size 10. They didn't know what a true 5'9", size 16 model was or how to fit her. They always called to ask, "Why did you send me someone this big?" I would send them the size they requested, but they would always answer with, "But, I just wanted someone a little bit bigger."

It took me four years to educate stylists, photographers and clients about size. For years, they phoned up and asked what a size 16 model looked like, or a size

18, 20 or 26. Sometimes they would call back and tell me the model I sent was too skinny.

While all this was happening, I was becoming more and more comfortable in my surroundings. All of a sudden the world from sizes 4 to 10 didn't exist for me. I started to look at my world as sizes 12 to 26. Anyone outside that world was almost abnormal. *They* were the odd ones.

I would look at a size 12 to 14 model and think she was incredibly thin — not dissimilar to how a size 2 would look at a regular agency. A size 26 model looked fine to me, because I was about that size at the time. A size 20 model was average.

This was something I knew well, something I had already bought into. I was very familiar with it. I was a product of my own environment, and my environment was something I not only agreed with and liked, but understood and believed in.

This was probably the best experience I ever had. I knew these women could use my help to adopt a healthy mental outlook on life. It brought a smile to my face every time I sent a model out for her first booking. Of course, she would be self-conscious and frightened of rejection at first, but she would come back pleased with herself. And, with time, I would see that same model go out for continuous bookings and not even think about her body size. If that's what it took to make a woman believe in who she was, then I would play my small part. Although my journey had been long, I always wanted to shorten the trip for others.

When I stopped being a model to become a modelling agent, and soon after a clothing designer and boutique owner as well, I was free once again to view my body for myself and no one else. It was a relief not to have to be a certain size. It was another breath of fresh air. I was able, once more, to ask myself what I wanted, which helped considerably.

However, the experience of being a model—at the time one of the only plus-size models, which was why I went up and down the dress-size rack—distorted the image in the mirror. I think even today I still have a slightly distorted image. Regardless of where I fall in the plus-size range, I consistently see a size 24 in the mirror. Although I see roundness and softness, it's always a size 24. It's not that I don't like what I see, it's that my vision is still a little blurred.

But then, in our culture it's not easy to see entirely clearly. It's unfortunate, but we are seen and judged at such a superficial level. Unless you've really experienced something substantial in your life, it's very difficult to detect depth in someone else. It's usually the people who haven't experienced trauma, those whose lives are smooth as glass, who are superficial. And these are the people who seem to dictate how the rest of us should be feeling.

Beauty truly is in the eye of the beholder, but it's not easy to expose that belief to everyone else—we all seem afraid of what other people may think. Besides, we have other high standards to adhere to—we must be beautiful and we must be wealthy. Unfortunately (or fortunately), there are a lot of truly beautiful people in the world who just can't afford to play this silly game.

The reality is, in our culture, everyone seems afraid of putting a stop to the game. Not only are we scared of what the other guy will think, we're frightened of who we really are, frightened that we might not measure up.

We're afraid we'll be rejected by the other players for not playing by the rules.

For quite a bit of my life, I followed someone else's ideals, trying to acquire someone else's ideals. Each attempt at freedom from those rules built my process from within. My own process was the determination to surround myself with comfortable situations in which my size was accepted, and travelling companions who stayed on the same road as me—a road of acceptance, a road to the land of the guilt-free.

I was able to do this by believing in myself. I was able to do it by proving my beliefs to others, by helping those in the same situation believe in themselves, and by living my life to the fullest, surrounded by these beliefs.

TWO

The Journey to Self-Esteem

WHY IS THE PINNACLE of success a big house, big car, big boat and a big ring on a thin woman? I could never understand this. It was an incomprehensible fact that devastated my life.

During my first marriage, my husband was constantly out of work, quitting job after job. I was constantly worried. I was not only a big wife—and punished for that —I had a world of problems spinning inside my head. I fretted about the rent, I was bothered by bills, I agonized over whether Gus would find work, and I worried that I wasn't good enough. My whole life tended to be one big worry.

I anticipated the worst, but at the same time, I was always waiting for that magical day when I would be thin. I thought my family and friends would accept me then, and I would be happier. My husband's abuse would stop, and everything would be perfect. The brink of my happiness was riding on that day.

In the meantime, however, I tried to find some form of acceptance. Years of searching for approval from everyone around me only deflated my poor self-image. I was so submissive to everything and everyone in my life. I wanted to be accepted. I just had to be accepted. I tried to grab hold of love and affection whenever I could, even if the only way was to initiate it myself.

I became a "yes" person, a nurturing woman, one who was always doling out caring advice — all for the sole purpose of getting a thank you, a compliment or a hug in return.

But, it didn't take long to realize the only way I would be emotionally well-nourished was if I fed myself. It was a revelation that made me angry, and made me eat all the more. It was the only nurturing I could find. It was the only hug available. Food seemed to understand me. It filled me; it filled the void.

Food comforted me, consoled me and became very familiar and rewarding. I rewarded myself and punished my husband with it. At a deeper level, however, I found I also punished myself by eating too much. Food became my friend, my lover and my enemy. I couldn't and wouldn't give it up.

The end result was always punishment. I still wasn't acceptable. I had stepped onto a carousel that never stopped — nobody would accept me because I ate, but food had now become my crutch.

I thought I still liked who I was, and yet I was constantly succumbing to other people's needs and wants. I felt like an imposter.

I began to withdraw from society, my family and friends. I stopped trusting people. I became moody and reclusive.

Looking back now, it seemed to happen quite suddenly. But if I trace back a little further, I can see the beginnings of self-doubt.

At eighteen, when I was pregnant with Philip, I really didn't realize that my self-esteem was starting to fray. Being pregnant was so important to me. And having a child so young, I suppose I was excited by the prospect of playing house. I wanted everyone to see I was pregnant, not only because of the significance it held to me, but for the importance it held for our families.

I noticed a difference when my body started to grow; in fact, I had a feeling I was weighing more than I should have. But, it didn't concern me that much; there was a very good reason for it.

Months before Philip was due, I had a check-up with my doctor. After all the testing, he told me I had toxemia, and he wanted me admitted to the hospital.

When I checked into the hospital they took down the usual statistics and weighed me. I remember getting on the scale for the very first time since becoming pregnant. I didn't know numbers could go that high. I never dreamt I could weigh more than two hundred pounds. When the arrow pointed to 240, I was overwhelmed and astonished. I felt so huge, so obese and so ashamed.

I felt totally alone. I was too embarrassed and afraid to share it with my husband. Part of the shame was not understanding what that number meant. It just seemed like I was walking into a big, black hole. It was another place. I was leaving one world and entering another. Not only was I becoming a mother, everything was changing.

I was shocked by that number, but added to that were the unpleasant things that had already started to happen. People had started saying things like, "You're getting so big, how many months along are you?" "How much weight have you put on? You must be carrying an awfully big baby!"

I knew I was gaining a lot of weight. I was beginning to feel large and lethargic. I didn't know what was happening to my body. It was almost as if I was another person. I didn't understand the image in the mirror or the feelings I had looking into it. I didn't understand why I was becoming this person. I didn't even look like me. I felt uncomfortable.

Maybe it was the look of disapproval on the nurse's red face when I stood on the scale; maybe it was the way she gasped. But, finally, I was beginning to understand.

The doctor told me I was gaining too much weight. It was because of this, he said, I had developed toxemia. Not only was I out of control, in their eyes, I was also harming what was inside me—the baby.

It was most definitely the first time I felt so clearly devalued, but it wasn't the first time I felt big. Just before our honeymoon, I weighed about one hundred and forty-five pounds. At this time, I had my first encounter with Gus's mother. She had arrived home from a lengthy trip abroad. I remember the first thing she said when I met her: "You're such a beautiful girl, but you're a big girl."

That "but" confused me. She was obviously a kind woman, and I could tell she liked me; however, that "but" told me something else. Maybe she thought I was too big for Gus. Maybe I wasn't the perfect image she had of a new bride for her only son. Or maybe I wasn't what she pictured me to be. It was another negative thought planted in my head.

Actually, there were a few other subtle messages along the way that made me feel insecure before I stood on that scale.

Back when I was a young teen, about thirteen, I began receiving attention from men. Boys were different; I knew how to handle their attentions. This attention was coming from grown men—and it was not only strange, it was ghastly.

In particular, I was receiving attention from a certain friend of the family. It started out as overt friendliness, which didn't alarm me at first; I was a friendly child. However, it didn't stop there. There were times when this man wanted to put his head in my lap. This seemed odd and unnatural to me, but he was a friend of the family, someone everyone else trusted, so I acquiesced. I didn't want to appear rude for my family's sake. However, he didn't reciprocate that kind of concern.

One night, after I had gone to bed, he came to my room. He started with soft words and escalated to fondling. I was just a child and it frightened me, sickened me and shocked me into believing there was something wrong with my body. I associated his sickness with my newly growing form. And from that moment on, I was not only intimidated by my own sexuality, I began to feel unsure of myself as a person and as a woman.

The experience started a mental distortion of my body and a decrease of self-esteem. I was confused into thinking that to be truly accepted by my family and the people we knew, I had to somehow be less attractive than I was. I didn't want to hurt anyone's feelings or make anyone feel uncomfortable—and I didn't want to feel guilty. I wanted to be accepted by everyone. I was too young to realize it was his problem, nothing was wrong with me. I was too young to realize I could have told someone about it. I felt immense guilt for something someone else had done to me.

Later, as a teenager, there were moments I felt tremendous pride in my body and myself. However, when those moments arose — and they arose often — they were coupled with that same sense of guilt. It made me feel like a freak. It made me stop and think. I didn't want how I looked or how I acted to disrupt anything in my life.

When I met Gus, during my years at high school, it was my appearance that got his attention. I would visit his family's restaurant, where he worked part-time. I would make sure he was cooking on those days, and I would dress nicely for the occasion. It was how we met.

When we dated, we constantly argued. We broke up so many times, usually over my appearance. He was always examining the way I looked. I was criticized for dressing too provocatively — my skirt was too short, my top was too low, or the whole outfit was just too tight. Or I might have glanced at someone too long, or maybe my knees weren't pressed together tightly enough. I was always doing something wrong.

He wanted this perfect little girl. I tried to be perfect, but once again I was too pretty and my body was too appealing. I couldn't just be an attractive young woman and feel the way I wanted to feel. I was constantly scrutinized. And, he was slowly trying to change everything about me.

When I became pregnant, it almost seemed like a godsend. It seemed like a bridge between being thin and unacceptable to being large and possibly acceptable. I wasn't sure. Not that this was the reason I got pregnant, but in my heart I hoped it was a bridge.

I thought if being thin meant being taken advantage of, or disliked and scrutinized, then maybe being big would make people open their arms and accept me. Maybe that way I wouldn't be a threat. There was a dim hope that maybe this was the answer.

From that moment on, I experienced a very big personal battle for self-esteem that continued for years. In fact, the word self-esteem gives what happened too much dignity. I didn't even know it existed. Self-esteem was too much of a grown-up term, a word used by university graduates.

What I felt was similar to being in a dark dungeon, a place where you can't even begin to understand self-esteem. When you're young and naive, you've never even heard of the word. What I had was despair, a feeling of not knowing anything more than the sense of a damp, dark tunnel. It was where you felt you deserved to be put down, ignored and even punished for not measuring up to the standards of others. If you didn't conform to their image of ideal, then you were nothing more than what they treated you as.

Self-respect didn't exist. I was constantly busy trying to please. I did anything to satisfy others, whether it be serving my husband dinner in front of the television or making sure the kitchen floors were scrubbed and shiny. This way, I thought I wouldn't be under scrutiny for anything more than my body. I had to be perfect in every other way; I became an excellent housekeeper and an excellent cook. I created things I could be praised for, because I knew I wouldn't be complimented on my looks. I had to find other ways to be looked at, as someone who made a difference somehow—even if it was just through housework.

Bringing up Philip became the prime aspect of my life, because I was always complimented on how I was raising him and how he was turning into a fine young boy. It got to a point where if Philip disappointed me, I became angry with him. He had become an extension of me. I was so selfish. He became proof of how terrific I was. When he acted up or got angry, I took it as a personal reflection. It upset me all the more that his behaviour might take away the few compliments of being a good mother.

I never understood what self-esteem was. I understand it now, I can diagnose it, but at that time I didn't know there was such a thing. I knew I felt differently from how I felt before. I had been a young, lively, beautiful girl who didn't have a care in the world, just a wide, open future. I had become a young woman who was being controlled by everyone and was submissive to the control, just to be accepted. I wanted so desperately to be loved, nurtured and cared for.

I didn't dare go back to being that lively, young girl. I was frightened that returning to her would bring back the rejection of being attractive. I had already had enough bad experiences being young and lively. My need to be needed and my want to be wanted were much greater than my need to be a sexual young woman. Although people seemed unhappy with who I had become, I thought it was the only route available to approval. So I kept plodding.

But, of course, after a few submissive and grueling years I began to get very angry. I realized I was indeed a human being with god-given rights, and there was only so much I could take. There are only so many ways people can trample over you. I came to the understanding that no matter how hard I tried, I couldn't please everyone. If I didn't eat, they weren't happy; if I did eat, they weren't happy; if I wasn't what they wanted, they weren't happy; if I wanted to be myself, they weren't happy. If I did everything I was supposed to do—wash the floors, clean the house, look after Philip, go on diets, cook the food—they still weren't happy. I still wasn't good enough.

No matter what I did, it wasn't good enough. When was good good enough? The anger was swelling inside me, almost like a tea kettle boiling—violently boiling—with its whistle going off. But no one was listening. No one was paying that kind of attention to me.

When my husband became verbally and physically abusive, I knew it wasn't going to get better. I had nothing to lose by fighting back. At a certain point in my life, I had believed I deserved everything because I wasn't what he wanted me to be—I hadn't tried hard enough to be that person.

Some people behave because they don't want to be reprimanded; children behave because they don't want to be spanked. But I was being reprimanded; I was being beaten. What did I have to lose? My life? I wanted to die anyway. I was tired of being this thing. I wasn't even a human being anymore. I was a thing. I was a vent for them. And as far as a lot of people were concerned, I didn't have a heart, I didn't have feelings, I wasn't anything.

Of course, my family loved me, but by this time they were away from me. They lived hundreds of miles away from the city. And I never told them what was happening. If they called to say they were coming for a visit and I had visible marks of abuse, I'd tell them I was going away for the weekend and wouldn't be home. I didn't phone my mother when I was upset, because I didn't want her to know. I was too embarrassed.

I know my lowest ebb was when I tried to think of ways to end it. I used to lie awake at night and contemplate various forms of suicide. I thought there was no other possible way of getting out. I felt doomed.

I'd always believed in the saying, "You make your bed, you lie in it." My bed was made, but unfortunately its sheets were never washed, and it was getting dirtier and dirtier. And I didn't know how to get out of it.

The only reason I had to keep going was that little baby I had brought into the world. The only reminder that my life was worth living was Philip. I had a responsibility to take care of him. I couldn't give up.

The only other reason I had to get up in the morning was to go to school. By this point, I had signed up for university classes in order to get the education I had set aside to have my child. To me it was just another duty, but it was a different world, and it provided a glimmer of hope.

I certainly could have decided not to go to school. Going was not easy. But why sit around and wait? It was very hard to wait, when you felt like you were about to be executed. If you have a chance to go out and enjoy the fresh air one more time, before they put the bag over your head and the noose around your neck, you do it.

Going to school, if anything, was my salvation (apart from my son). It was the only breath of air available, be it stale or not. Still, I questioned myself daily about what I was doing. "What am I doing here? Who am I trying to fool? I'm too stupid, so why am I here? Where am I going with this?"

I felt horrible at school. Many times I had to wear sunglasses to hide black eyes, or I felt sick over what had happened the night before or over what might happen that night. When classes were over, I used to run out of school, afraid to miss the bus, terrified I'd be five minutes late getting home. I was constantly worried that something drastic was going to happen.

Living on pins and needles was exhausting. You get to a point where you're so full of frustration and failure for not fulfilling everyone else's demands. But you also can only kick a dog so much, before it turns around and bites you. You can only be so mean, before that dog walks the street. I knew my out was not suicide; I had to live this life. If I was going to live it, I had to start fighting back somehow.

God knows I had a reason to fight back, and by this time I had also found the encouragement to try. By chance, I had met a woman named Darlene. Darlene and I were living parallel lives and, because of that, we could understand each other, share things with each other, including friendship. We were the best of friends.

Meeting someone who empathized, understood and liked me as a person, regardless of my size, reassured me that I was right to be who I was, and supported the idea that I had a right to fight for that.

Darlene became so significant that I never spoke about her to anyone. I didn't think it would do her justice. I didn't even speak about her to my husband, because I thought it would have made our friendship seem less than it was. She wouldn't have been significant to Gus at all. It was very important to him that people I knew or met were attractive. They had to look good. If he knew I was friends with someone heavier than I was, he wouldn't approve. But she was worth much more than what he would have thought. I wasn't searching for his approval of her. She didn't need approval, she was a person—a whole person. I didn't want him to touch that by failing to appreciate her whole worth. So I kept our friendship to myself. And, it was probably the most selfish thing I had ever done.

Darlene gave me incentive to speak up. I think Gus was pretty surprised the first time I said, "Leave me alone!" I think he started to realize there wasn't a hope in hell of changing me anymore. And I think it scared him.

When you're submissive and you allow people to vent their anger at you, it gives them a small ray of hope that you may become the person they want to mold you into. But when you start fighting back, they start losing that hope. As Gus started to lose hope, he started to stray. He stopped coming home at night.

There were many nights Philip and I were left alone; many mornings when we woke up alone. I knew Gus had found someone else. Of course, this hurt, but my self-worth had nowhere else to go—it was already on the ground. I was face down in the dirt.

He had found the woman I wasn't, the thin, attractive woman he always wanted. And, obviously, that made all the difference in the world to him. That was the reality of his beatings and his abusive attitude toward me.

But, in a way, I was almost satisfied that he had found someone else and was leaving me alone. He had found another cause. Now, maybe I could get up on my knees, even up on my feet, before being kicked back down. Before this moment, trying to get up seemed like such a difficult step—someone was always standing over me, making sure I didn't budge. If I was left alone, I might be able to discover who I was, maybe even learn to like myself. And maybe I could become strong enough to start living again.

I hadn't been living. I had been existing. There's a big difference between the two. I had been existing from moment to moment. There wasn't a future. How can you have a future, when you live like a caged animal? I didn't want to go out and Gus didn't want to take me out; in his eyes, I wasn't good enough to go out—anywhere. I wasn't even good enough to go downstairs to the laundry room. I felt horrible. Why would I want to do anything? Why would I want to go anywhere?

Self-esteem? I actually thought what I was living was what life was all about. I didn't know what life was. But I knew I had to get up from the dirt. I wanted to breathe. I wanted to figure out, in my own mind, if there was a reason to keep on going.

Devastated by what was happening, knowing my husband was having an affair, I felt sick to my stomach constantly. I knew something had to happen, but I was so scared. I guess I had looked at Gus in the same way I looked at food. Even though I knew what it was doing to me, I was afraid to let it go. Even though I was being abused, it was still a form of attention. It was sick, but it was true.

His affair was a form of abandonment, but with time came a feeling of peace. I was now able to look at my son and be a mother. I shifted my focus. I was able to love Philip unconditionally. I never again based any decisions for him on what Gus would have wanted. In the past, my concerns for Philip included what his father would have wanted—what wouldn't make his father angry. I began basing decisions on how I felt.

I started to think for myself, and it began through Philip. I was proud of the decisions I made for my son, and I never discussed them with his father. This was a stepping stone in itself.

At this time I was willing to let my husband go. However, he didn't want to go. He had changed his mind. He wanted to keep both his wife and his lover. I said no and goodbye.

The night the marriage ended, I cried myself to sleep and woke up alone. I shipped Philip off to his grandmother's and, at a friend's suggestion, I went to a retreat run by nuns.

I spent five days there. I spoke to the priests and nuns about my life and where it could be going. I began to realize that this was the path I was chosen to follow. And no matter what happened or would happen, something good always comes from something horrid. They helped me realize that if you believe in yourself, you can conquer all. So I decided whatever happened, I was going back to the city to make the best of what I had.

I knew I had two weeks left on my rent. After that, I would owe $750. I didn't have a job. I didn't have any money. I didn't know how I was going to look after the two of us, but I had to.

The odd thing was I never thought of myself when the marriage ended. On automatic pilot, I thought about how I was going to keep a roof over our heads, what we were going to eat, and how we would survive. But, just as quickly, it dawned on me that even if we had very little to eat, even if we had to huddle together under a tent, it would be okay. Philip and I were going to be safe.

My mother brought down a care package that would feed Philip and I for a few weeks. I spoke to the people in charge of the building where we lived and told them about our situation. They told me about another apartment building that had just been built. I would have cheaper rent there, but I would have to volunteer my services.

And that's what we did. We moved. I was a lifeguard in the summer; during the winter months I taught a stretch and aerobics class. I was more than two hundred pounds and teaching aerobics. I had to do it. You do whatever you can to survive.

I found a grain of self-esteem when I was forced to step outside of my apartment. I knew I had no other choice but to get out there and do something. I had to do it for the two of us.

And, at that time, it was pretty much just the two of us. I didn't have many friends, because I didn't want anyone getting too close. I was used to a very solitary life.

That first summer, with university closed, I focused on my lifeguard job. At the pool, I started to meet other mothers. We would occasionally go out for coffee; very occasionally we went out in the evening. It was different for me. I didn't exactly feel like I fit in; I was unfamiliar with socializing and I was larger. But meeting these women gave me the experience of getting out and doing something different.

Through gaining a few friends, I started to slowly develop self-esteem. I realized I was capable of making friends, something I hadn't been sure I could do. Through meeting other women and building friendships, I eventually met that woman in the mirror. It was a slow process, but it too was something I hadn't discovered before.

The time I spent alone was put to good use. I started to do things I never appreciated before. Going from a childhood home with many siblings into a marriage that crowded me (not with companionship, but with expectations and demands), I never had much time to do what I wanted. The simple pleasures of reading a book or listening to music were not just simple pleasures. They became wonderful, meaningful pastimes. I learned so much by coming in contact with myself, realizing I was worth a hell of a lot more than I had previously believed.

I started to look at my life as a ray of hope. My schooling became very important. My son was of paramount importance. And I was becoming increasingly important to me.

THREE

Sticks and Stones

I KNOW NOW that negative comments from the outside world began the day I let my guard down. When I realized I was different from other people, that I didn't look the same, I started to hear their words. And because I desperately wanted to be the same, I accepted the insults and let them affect my everyday life.

These comments began, of course, when I became significantly bigger. When I was twenty or thirty pounds overweight, there was barely a word. But after I had added fifty pounds to my body, the insults grew. They came not only from complete strangers, but also from family. They surfaced soon after I had gained weight around the time my son was born. My mother would say, "You have to lose weight. Your dad and I are very concerned for you."

I knew my mother was concerned; in fact, she was concerned about a lot of things. We had a habit of going for drives in the country. When she picked me up, she'd say, "Jackqueline, don't sit in the back. You'll ruin the rear shocks." This was by no means an intentional slander; she honestly believed I would harm the car. But it hurt me to think she felt I was that big, and that she would say so without considering my feelings.

On occasions when we were celebrating around the table, my father would pass around seconds or dessert and say, "Don't give that to Jackqueline, she doesn't need it." They never asked me if I was hungry. But then I never looked at it as a food issue, anyway. To me, they were leaving me out. They were ignoring me because I wasn't important enough. I took their meaning much deeper and further than simply holding back a cookie.

I knew my parents were trying to help me in their own way. But I also knew they were looking at me through fuzzy lenses, and this prepared me for what would happen in the outside world. My parents were doing it, my husband was doing it—I thought the outside world had permission to make comments, too.

If the people who loved me felt it necessary to say things, then maybe I really was interfering with other people's lives. If I was as pretty as they said, maybe it was my responsibility to lose weight and make a more attractive picture for them. Maybe I had been taking up too much space.

It was the beginning of a build-up of insecurities, and a resignation to cruel and unacceptable treatment. There were so many times I nodded my head in agreement, hung it in shame, or shook it in disbelief that people could be so cruel and yet so kind at the same time. "You're so beautiful. If only you weren't so morbidly obese," they seemed to be saying.

I dealt with so many backhanded compliments. It seemed completely natural to be hurt and loved at the same time. I thought I was supposed to be treated that way, because I was different. Because people like me were a menace and a shame to society, we weren't to show ourselves until we could be revealed in the purest of light and the fittest of form.

And so it began. I was taken at face value by those in the inner sanctum, and eventually by those in the outside world.

Looking back, it's clear that I not only allowed the remarks, I looked for them. In the outside world, I would watch people and wait for their reactions, or I would stop as they passed me in the street and turn my head to see if they were turning to look at me.

It was bizarre behaviour, but it was all based on tremendous guilt and an overwhelming urge to apologize for not conforming to society's strict image of beauty. I knew I could have been prettier or thinner, and because I wasn't, I thought people had permission to say things. And I waited for them.

The pain those comments caused became an impetus to look harder at myself. It forced me into hiding, where I would dwell on my body. Without the insults, I feared I would just continue to be happy and continue to gain weight. I thought I needed outside comments as a tool, because I used them as a constant reminder for change. So I went out of my way to get hurt.

I'd actually trap people into it. During conversations, I'd blurt out, "I can't believe I haven't eaten today," leaving the field wide open for someone to snicker, "*You* haven't eaten today? Right."

I was constantly setting myself up like the straight man in a bad comic routine, with every punch-line forcing me to change. Sometimes the nasty remarks would compel me to diet, but usually I'd fail. I was setting myself up for failure at every turn—the acceptance of hurtful phrases, the slim chances of diet success, and the inevitable negative image of myself. I felt like a complete failure all around.

The only positive aspect this twisted behaviour brought was strength. The constant barrage of punches left me harder. There came a point when I finally realized I had to begin to protect myself. I couldn't bear another miserable day filled with self-hate. This huge neon sign read, "STOP!" I could see myself on a slow motion ride to suicide. I couldn't feel the pain anymore. I was numb.

I decided I didn't want to succumb to anyone else's feeling of worth. I wanted to be worth something, but *I* wanted to decide what that was. I was going to cut loose anything that tied me to anger, anguish or feelings of incompetence. Of course, my first husband was one of the most obvious tangles, but there were others. I let go of any physical or emotional abuse. I was stepping into a new life.

I was going to fight for my own beliefs, but not because I was so wrapped up in conceit for who I thought I was—I didn't have any conceit. The only thing I had was a cornerstone to build from, which was inscribed, "Enough is enough."

I thought, "I am worth a little bit more. I have to be." I had had all the boyfriends in high school, the top grades. I had been on the track and field team and had a box full of music awards. I had been so physical and active. How did I become this way?

It wasn't until I sat down and analyzed it that I understood I hadn't been that way because of physical prowess, but mental prowess. Sure, I could do much more physically than I had allowed myself, but more to the point, I could do so much more emotionally. I'd let people pommel me and convince me I couldn't do any better.

So, instead of turning around and looking to see if people were watching me in the street, I would pass them with a wide smile on my face and a hello. I was frightened to death at the beginning, expecting responses like, "Please, I don't talk to fat people," or "I can't believe you have the nerve to speak to me." But I was ready for the criticism. If it came my way, this time I was determined to come at it in a different direction.

If I felt badly about a comment, it was now because I was too wrapped up in myself to realize it wasn't my problem. How conceited could I be to think that it would be my fault that someone else was being rude and cruel? Instead, I began to think, "Wow, do they have a big problem. I'm wonderful. Why are they speaking that way? Staring like that?"

My whole psychological approach began to evolve. I wanted to start educating other people, even if it was on a vigilante basis. I wanted to go out there and stop everyone I could from insulting me, knowing that if I could spare just one large-sized woman I would have accomplished something. Now, instead of looking for comments to hurt me, I went out to find them and correct them.

If someone gave me a strange look, I'd say, "Hi, do I know you? You just gave me a strange look." I would hit the problem head on. In most cases, people were completely dumbfounded that I had the guts to approach them. They were shocked that I had no insecurity about myself, because in most cases they did—which is why they made the comments in the first place. They'd usually laugh out of surprise. I would laugh, too. The next thing you knew, we'd be laughing at the situation together. Of course, it took courage to stand up for myself, but I've always believed that courage is just fear that has said its prayers.

Once, long ago, Peter and I went to dinner with a close friend and her date, who happened to be a policeman. While we were walking to the restaurant, the policeman yelled out to someone across the street. It was another cop, a buddy of his who was on the beat.

The other policeman yelled, "Who's the big unit you're with?"

I thought I heard him correctly, but I wasn't sure. "Did you say something to me?" I asked as we approached him.

"I was just wondering who you were," he answered.

"You just called me a unit."

"I was only joking," he mumbled.

"You just called me a unit," I repeated.

"Oh, relax," he laughed. "You *are* a big unit. What's the big deal?"

I was flabbergasted. This civil servant, this man whose job it was to serve and protect the public, was certainly not serving or protecting me. More to the point, he didn't even seem to care or understand.

To make my point very clear, I went to the police station and filled out a formal complaint. The offending officer was called in to make amends. It was quite surreal; he was at least 350 pounds himself. In the end, he apologized. I still see him out on the beat. We wave. We chat. What's more important, however, was getting satisfaction in this case. I was justified in complaining, and I was able to get a result.

Protecting myself became a hobby after awhile. I started to feel good. I had stopped feeling sorry for myself, and had begun to feel, "The hell with it. No one is pushing my buttons, unless I let them. I'm pushing my own buttons." If someone criticized me, I was damned well going to address it.

In fact, I was feeling so good, I decided to spread it around. I set out on a mission to hand out compliments. I knew if someone gave one to me it would make my day. Still, I made it a point to offer sincere compliments. I wouldn't just walk up to someone and say, "Great hat," "Nice nose job," or "Terrific biceps."

The Girl Guide in me came out, and I began helping people. Before you knew it, there were a whole group of us doling out kind words. I don't know how much of a difference I made, but I know I made a difference.

Adopting this attitude had a tremendous effect on my self-confidence and made me the person I am today. Now, I find it ironic that I spend my entire day talking about being fat and liking it. I've come full circle. Nonetheless, it wasn't an immediate change. It took time, it took persistence, and it took a lot of lessons.

Not long into my new found attitude, Peter and I went to the movies. Peter happens to be pretty particular about seating, so as he was searching for the right vantage point, I stood in the aisle waiting. I was holding all our snacks so he could have free reign of the theatre. I was standing with two of everything in my arms— popcorn, pop, Snickers, and more. As I was waiting, I scanned the audience. It didn't take long to realize there was a row of young people scanning me. There I was, a

250-pound woman loaded down with enough junk food for two. Some of them were laughing, some were nudging and pointing.

My head started to pound. My palms started to sweat. I started to panic. I didn't know what to do.

Peter came back to take me to our seats, but I had an urge to say something to these people before I moved on.

"Are you laughing at me?" I asked.

All of them gave me the same quizzical look.

"Are you laughing at me?" I repeated.

"Aren't you Jackqueline Hope from Big, Bold & Beautiful?" one said. "We just saw you on television yesterday."

I knew they had been staring at me and laughing, but I hadn't a clue it could be in recognition. At the time, I was the only person talking on television about being plus-size, and there I was holding all that junk food. Yes, it was funny—I would have laughed, too. But instead of thinking about all the possible reasons for their pointing and smiling, I was back to being a frightened big girl who was being teased right in front of her own eyes.

It only took a few moments, but I learned a lifelong lesson. Not all giggles and whispers are cruel.

With time, I learned to handle almost any situation. I use the word "almost" because I never quite mastered the ability to deal calmly with others being harassed. I learned to face the insults, and eventually there came a time when I faced the insults for those who weren't quite ready to deal with them themselves.

Years ago, a friend and I decided to end an afternoon with a couple of burgers. Both of us were big girls, each more than 250 pounds, but that in no way deterred us from eating in public.

Once inside the restaurant, I stopped to grab some matches, while she went ahead to get a table.

On her way through, I heard a comment from one of two men seated for lunch. "Seeing something like that turns me right off anything fattening. I'll have a salad with dressing on the side."

As I walked past, his companion spit out, "Ditto."

I turned and asked, "You two are sitting at a table for four?"

"Yeah. What's it to you?"

"Then," I said, "there's room for me."

When I pulled up a chair, one of them barked, "Excuse me?!"

"I don't know if I'll excuse you," I said. "You see that girl over there? She's my friend."

"She's not coming over here to sit down, too."

"No," I agreed. "She's too good to join you. She's a wonderfully sensitive person. I overheard what you said, and I know she heard it, too."

"What?" one asked, "about the salad?"

"Yes, about the salad. You want to talk about it?"

"No," they both responded, dismissing me with their scowls.

I continued anyway. "You know, it would have been none of my business if my friend hadn't heard."

Meanwhile, my friend was waiting at the other table, visibly embarrassed.

I turned my attention back to them. "Are you two lovers?"

"What?"

"You two are gay, are you not?"

"What's that got to do with anything?"

"Are you two gay?" I repeated.

"Yes."

"My point should be taken right now. You're gay. You lead your life the way you want. And if anyone opposes you, you're hurt. Am I right?"

"Yeah," one said. "So?"

"We live our lives the way we want to live. And when we come in for a burger, we don't think—we don't expect—people like you to be talking about us or insulting us."

"Lady, come on," one interrupted. "We didn't..."

"Yes, you did. You hurt my friend and you hurt me. How would you have felt if we had been sitting here as you two walked in, and I had said, 'Thank God I'm heterosexual. Who the hell would want to be gay?'"

"We'd have felt horrible."

We continued talking. My friend gave up waiting and, with my encouragement, came over. We joined them for lunch. To this day, we're friends.

Some people really are quite wonderful, they just speak before they think. I believe if people realized how much they hurt others, a good percentage would stop talking.

The old saying about sticks and stones is baloney. Names hurt. They can be devastating. But if you don't stand up to them—if you run from them as I used to—they become very similar to a bad relationship. You think, "All right, whatever. I just don't want to fight today." You become passive, because you're tired of arguing.

It takes a lot of energy to fight back, but it's worth it for your self-esteem. When you leave your point of view on a positive note, you've set an example of how people should be treated.

Nothing could feel better. It's like freeing a bird that's recovered from injury, releasing something that is completely innocent and hasn't harmed anyone in any way. Setting yourself free from hurtful messages and cruel innuendoes is being able to say, "This hurts. Let me go. I'm trying to mend myself. I'm trying to feel better about me. Yes, I'm large, and I know that you don't find it a pleasing picture, but I'm not hurting you. If you don't want to look, don't look. Look at something else. I am what I am. Let me be that. And, if changes should be made, let me be the one to decide."

There isn't a single person on this planet who has the right to step into someone else's life and decide what their ailment is, the cause of their problem, or how to cure it. But, of course, that doesn't stop some. In my travels I've found it's usually people who are bored with their own existences who find it necessary to delve into others' affairs. They are the ones who actually believe your appearance is their business. Well, advice is free and insults are free—the high cost involved is someone else's self-esteem. This world would be a much more productive place if all of us would divert our energies to things that can and will make a difference.

Obviously, each of us faces battles and lessons along the way. Some take tremendous energy and courage, but not all call for tenacity. Some can be entirely effortless and entertaining. On one particular day, when Peter and I were vacationing in the Bahamas, I stumbled across a treasure trove of enlightenment.

Instead of having a lounge-around-the-beach vacation, we decided to try some things we'd never done before. Peter came up with the idea of parasailing. I was a little self-conscious about my weight, but agreed anyway.

When we arrived at the parasailing hut, there was a sign that read, "Maximum weight 200 pounds, due to winds." I looked at Peter. Peter asked the attendant if the restrictions ever changed. The man looked at me and asked, "How much do you weigh?" "Two hundred and forty pounds," I answered. "No," he shook his head, "we never have a wind strong enough for that."

We shuffled down the beach to the glass-bottom boat rides. There we found another sign: "Maximum weight 300 pounds." Obviously, the only way we were going to see the bottom of the sea was if we went out separately. We decided against it.

Back at the hotel we came across yet another sign. This time it was for massages. It quoted different amounts of time at different prices. As Peter and I stood outside the door, deliberating between half an hour and hour-long massages, a Bahamian woman peered out to greet us.

"You. Big lady with big body," she stated. "No half hour. At least one hour."

At this point, Peter couldn't hold back the laughter. "Size isn't the issue here," he said. "Having a good time is. Let's do it."

Back out on the beach, with nowhere else to go (the winds hadn't picked up and the boats hadn't gotten any larger), we both flopped onto towels entirely relaxed from our hour-long massages.

It wasn't long before a young peddler came hawking T-shirts. I wasn't interested, but he wouldn't take no for an answer. Peter winked and whispered, "Tell him you're too big for them." I did, and off he trotted.

The next day I saw the same boy darting around the beach. He spotted me and came running. His arms were loaded with XX-large T-shirts, which read "Bahama Mama." I bought seven.

Obviously, I didn't have to go parasailing or sea combing to find something new. I found people really do look at you for what you are. Some, unfortunately, insult you, some compliment you, others observe and think before they speak.

That one day revealed we can be light about largeness. We don't have to be so serious, secretive and dark about being overweight. There can be a fun side, a flip side, a lighter side. Now I laugh along with others, as long as the humour is light and it's not insulting, because it is funny. No matter what you have that's different from the average run-of-the-mill Joe, it can be made light of. Humour lightens everybody's attitude, and makes those around you comfortable in knowing they don't have to walk on egg shells around you. You can be confident without being arrogant and full of yourself.

Laughter is entirely therapeutic, which is why I surround myself with people who can laugh—people who love me for who I am, have fun with me and appreciate my outlook.

In business, I try to change people who think they have the right to hurt others. That's my job. But I wouldn't be bothered to have people around me in my personal life whom I had to work on.

Today, my inner sanctum is full and happy. I am surrounded by close relationships that are built on mutual admiration and respect.

This, of course, includes my family. My parents are very complimentary now. They appreciate who I am. My mother took me aside a while back; she wanted me to know how proud she and Dad were of me. She said they'd recognized that I'd always been different, and how I was destined to be. At the time I remember thinking that they probably didn't know how to handle me when I was younger. I could empathize.

At one point, many years ago, I had written my parents a letter. It was never sent. The satisfaction came from knowing it could be. However, if I had mailed it, I knew I would have hurt them much more than they ever hurt me. If they had read it, they would have doubted that they had raised me as well as they thought, which they had. It had been a simple, therapeutic exercise for a woman of twenty-four, who was digging up feelings and confusion from the past. I knew giving it to them would have accomplished nothing of value.

You see, there comes a time when you realize it's not your problem. It's *his* problem or *her* problem. *They* have to deal with it. You don't have a problem; you only have a problem in their eyes. Even if you were to lose weight, even if you managed to slim down to a size 8, they'd still find something to point their fingers at.

I began to understand that my weight hadn't been in anyone's way. My parents probably had other problems; I was their outlet to vent. My ex-husband wasn't happy; I was his scapegoat.

Part of my growing experience was figuring out that if someone else could see something in you as wrong, there was a distinct possibility they would label it as the sole cause of their troubles. Humans find it very difficult to look at their own faults. It's much easier to pass the buck than deal with yourself.

But, of course, it took me a while to realize this. And this may explain why it was easy for me to give others compliments at first. I'd spent such a long time believing everyone around me was better and knew better.

This is also why I find it such a pleasant surprise that I'm the one getting the compliments now. And it happened simply because I spoke the truth.

When you talk from the heart, rather than from the head, it makes a difference. When you speak out about what really happens, how people treat you, and any dilemma, no matter how trivial, that's made you feel less of a person, these things count.

They matter not only to me, they matter to my friends and family. These are the people who have witnessed the journey, from start to today. They've seen me on my soap box. They've watched the advocate who spoke what she believed, and that's the basis of their admiration and respect.

My father likes to rib, "You're a small-town girl who made it big in the city." But, of course, making it big in the city doesn't mean the journey is complete. Keeping your beliefs and your self-esteem taut and trim is a perpetual process. And there are times when a whole audience is watching.

Not long ago, on a live television show, the host and I were discussing insults—how they can fly and how they can hurt. While we were talking, a reporter was on location at an exercise class at Big, Bold & Beautiful. The plan was to cut to the reporter in the middle of our conversation and show the class at work.

When they cut away, the host introduced the reporter and asked, "Can you hear me, Jack? What's happening down there?"

"Well, before I get into that," he answered, "I heard this great joke the other night.

"Why isn't it safe to make love to a big woman?"

"Why?" I butt in.

"Because you can get a nosebleed from the altitude!"

The host looked into the camera and immediately said, "And, we'll cut to commercial."

I couldn't believe he had said it. It was obviously a bad joke, but more importantly it was in bad taste.

The producer rushed over, panicked about how we were going to handle it. The host asked, "Should we address it?" I didn't know exactly how we would. "Look, I apologize for this situation," she offered. "Why don't you use this as an example of how to handle insults on the street?"

We didn't go back to the reporter. Instead, the host told the audience I had a comment to make.

"This is exactly what I've been talking about," I began. "What Jack just said happens to plus-size women every-day. There are women at home now who have been completely insulted..." And I continued to talk on the subject.

Although Jack apologized profusely, he never lived it down. Three months after the segment aired, the show won an award of excellence—and they brought us all in, including Jack, for champagne. I don't think I've ever seen anyone more embarrassed. He'd blown it. He'd made a wrong call. He'd learned a lesson.

Of course, he wasn't the only one who'd learned a lesson. It was also another learning experience for me. Something had been said, and once again I addressed it. And I did it simply because I have come to know so well that once you address something, you put it to bed—it doesn't fester.

FOUR

Healthy Minds, Healthy Bodies

THE GENERAL PRACTICE of treating the larger population has been a mishmash of fact, opinion and myth. Over the years, the medical profession never really seemed to understand what being large was all about. During the last few decades, a myriad of studies has examined what's wrong with being big. If you have ever opened a medical journal in the past twenty years and scanned these studies' lists of fat-related health hazards, that alone would have been cause to give you palpitations. Today, opinions are changing. Still, the documented risks and possible benefits of being overweight are just as controversial as ever. Even doctors think it's confusing. After years of researching obesity, dieting, and their possible risks, Dr. Linda McCargar, at the University of Alberta, says many medical professionals find "it's still a cloudy issue."

It's no wonder most of us find medical opinions not only confusing, but intimidating as well. However, if the

larger population is to accept their bodies and themselves, it's important that we understand and regard our
health. And considering the medical profession finds it
all a little cloudy, maybe it's time we took a little medical examination of our own.

Bare bones

There are a few bare facts about fat. Firstly, there seems
to be a general weight-gaining trend in various countries
around the world, regardless of our obsession with thin
body types or the billions we spend on diet programs.
In fact, in the U.S., the state of obesity has doubled in
the last hundred years. In Denmark, a recent study
showed excess weight in young men increased by 700
percent from 1960 to 1974 (while in previous years the
numbers remained constant).

Although there is increasing evidence to prove genet-
ics play a large role in obesity, reports also show that the
percentage of calories we consume from fat in our diets
has risen from 32 percent in 1910 to 43 percent during
the '80s, which in itself may be cause for enlargement.

The second fact concerns females. At the moment,
approximately one quarter to one third of North American women are considered overweight. And, I use the
word "considered" for the simple fact that many weight
charts still in use are based on biased population studies, an arbitrary concept of body frame, and include no
leeway for the effects of aging.

Which brings us right back to confusion. These restricting weight tables have actually fuelled the perplexity of
weight and health. It was not long after they were established, through the late '40s and into the '50s, that the
medical profession started to view extra weight as a dis-

ease. By the '60s, most doctors had begun weighing people as part of a standard medical exam. And, according to dietitian and nutritionist Gail Marchessault, it was at this time "people were expected to consciously control their appetite and body weight; physical features formerly regarded as natural."

The great debate

There are reams of reports that compare physical well-being and physical largeness. Tons, in fact. However they're not consistent. You'd be hard-pressed to find a few reports that completely agree with one another.

Nonetheless, starting off with what are considered risk factors, there seems to be a general consensus that with obesity comes a danger of cardiovascular and pulmonary disease; stroke; hypertension (especially in men); endometrial and breast cancer (among postmenopausal women); stress incontinence; infertility; increased risk of infection after surgery; diabetes (most notably in women, which also brings twice the risk of heart disease); gall-bladder disease; and complications during pregnancy. These dangers are more associated with weight gain in early adulthood than they are with the added pounds that come at an older age.

Of these risks, I have experienced three — the last three.

I gained more than one hundred pounds during my pregnancy. At the time, I contracted toxemia. During delivery, I had to be given four epidurals to effectively eliminate pain. In the months that followed, I was weak and nauseated, and to this day my lower back gives me grief.

In 1993, at the age of thirty-seven, I was diagnosed as a diabetic, and by 1995 I had developed gallstones.

In each case, I was told by physicians that the illnesses were brought on not just by weight gain, but also by fluctuating body weight and fluctuating eating patterns.

And this is part of the great debate—excess weight is not the sole cause of health risks. In fact, many now view certain hazards, once attributed to excess weight, as actually caused by trying to lose weight. In one report, it was uncovered that "a 25 percent death rate among 200 obese men who lost weight by fasting was interpreted by the researchers as a hazard of obesity."

Dieting can be dangerous to your health. Not only can it have the unexpected outcome of added pounds, there are studies that indicate dieting can cause the same effects as extra weight—hypertension is one; mortality is another. One research group found a higher death rate for men who lost weight than for those who maintained a stable weight throughout adulthood—and this was for all causes of death, except cancer.

For women, the risks of dieting are just as pronounced. Society's bewildering battle for thinness has encouraged a slew of abnormal eating patterns—compulsive eating, bingeing, purging and fasting. These hold their own dangers.

The added danger with these eating habits is a risk of developing more serious health problems, namely bulimia nervosa and anorexia nervosa. Ninety-five percent of people suffering from these disorders are women.

Starvation diets bring along the probability of hypotension (low blood pressure); hypothermia; stunting of growth for young women; fractures similar to, but less serious than, osteoporosis; as well as depression, diminished libido and sleeping difficulties.

Bulimia, with its episodes of bingeing and purging, also holds a possibility of kidney damage, dehydration, seizures, gastrointestinal disturbances and general weakness.

Which only proves severe dieting is an unrealistic way to get healthy.

It is now believed that a modest drop in weight can result in substantial benefits. Recent studies show just a 10 percent reduction of body weight can normalize blood pressure and improve heart-related and diabetes health risks, among others. One study in particular proved losing 10 percent of body weight reduced health risks in 90 percent of obese patients.

Along with a more realistic view of weight loss, researchers are also finding excess weight has some surprising benefits of its own. There is proof that added pounds protect against death in premenopausal breast, lung, stomach and colon cancer in women, and lung and stomach cancer in men; and can be beneficial in osteoporosis, anemia, peptic ulcers, and respiratory and infectious diseases. There are also studies that show above-average weight is associated with maximum longevity.

Even though hard-and-fast rules about weight and health have yet to be ironed out, Dr. McCargar finds the pressure to focus on the scale "may have a greater effect on mental parameters. In that sense, it may be better to stay at the weight your body wants. If it's not the image society wants, it doesn't matter."

Thoughtful points
There is most definitely merit in staying at the weight your body desires, rather than the weight society admires. Not only does it deserve merit, it deserves applause. In

our culture, it's an achievement to hold fast to your individual beliefs.

It has been written that "the fat person's major handicap may not be his or her obesity, but the view that society takes of it."

This view starts early. Reports have shown that children as young as six see their overweight peers as stupid and less likeable. However, children aren't the only ones who can be cruel and ignorant. One study found many physicians described their obese patients as ugly and weak-willed; of these, quite a few doctors stated that they didn't believe their patients' assertions of trying to lose weight. In another study, mental health workers judged a psychological report more negatively when the file included a picture of an obese woman than they did when it included a photo of a slimmer female.

It's no wonder we can be intimidated by going to the doctor; it's no surprise that many of us, unfortunately, avoid or postpone appointments.

As Marchessault says, "Like the binding of Chinese women's feet, excessive attention on appearance can limit women's development."

A clean bill of health

To remedy the situation, a variety of government health departments, physicians and community health centres are developing more healthy goals.

The Body Mass Index (BMI) is one, and it's currently being adapted by many health professionals. The BMI was created to acknowledge a wide variety of body shapes and sizes as acceptable. Thankfully, it's quite simple and can be used by both men and women (with the exclusion of those younger than twenty or older than sixty-five).

The BMI uses height and weight measurements to calculate healthy weight zones. (To calculate your BMI, divide your weight in kilograms by your height in metres squared.) A BMI of less than 20 can be associated with health problems. BMIs that range from 20 to 27 are considered acceptable: those between 20 and 25 are felt to be a satisfactory weight for most people; those between 25 and 27 may lead to health difficulties for some individuals. A BMI of more than 27, however, is connected with an increasing risk of health hazards.

Where a 5' 6" woman could have weighed between 114 and 146 pounds on the old 1959 weight charts, or between 120 and 159 pounds according to the 1989 ideal, the BMI sets a healthy range at anywhere from about 125 to 173 pounds.

Another dose of good medicine is the more modern approach currently being taken by some toward healthy body images. The Canadian ministry of health, Health Canada, is one body with a healthy attitude. In a recent paper, it was noted that a shift must be taken "from weight to other goals, such as healthy eating, enjoyable physical activity and positive body image."

As well, it pointed out to health professionals that "the cardinal principle then, in the development of a weight strategy, must be 'if you cannot help, at least do not harm.' Policy makers must be absolutely sure that strategies will improve individual well-being, rather than exacerbate the prevailing prejudice against fatness."

In other words, it's time to measure what's important, and leave what's not so important alone. For years, our bodies and our fat-per-square-inch were the only things scrutinized. However, being healthy is not simply a physical thing, it's a mental state as well. If our self-esteem isn't intact, quite simply, we won't feel good. It's true a healthy body is important, but it's also true that if you're healthy in your mind, your body will follow.

FIVE

Setting a Place for Food

WHEN I WAS YOUNGER, food wasn't a very important aspect of my life. It wasn't a crutch. It wasn't something I could hide behind. It was survival. I competed in track and field and gymnastics in school. Food was simply fuel for my body, a necessity of life.

Actually, it was an inconvenience. In my teens, eating was something I *had* to do. "If you don't clear your plate," I can hear my mother saying, "you're not going out tonight." I knew if I didn't empty my plate or eat all my vegetables, there would be discipline. So I ate — or fed it to Princess, our dog. But food was not an all-consuming concern. It was only an issue when I sat down to it three times a day.

When I became pregnant at eighteen, I was one hundred and fifty pounds, very fit and very proud. My father-in-law was ecstatic. I held the only hope for carrying on the legacy of his family name. It was a happy time, and I was more than eager to boast of my coming arrival.

I would stick out my stomach and pretend I was more pregnant than I was. I bought maternity clothes in my first month. It was the first and last time I tried to be big.

I wanted to expand, and the only way I knew how was to eat. The more I ate, of course, the more I expanded. During the first six months of pregnancy I had gained about sixty pounds.

At the time, my husband owned a restaurant, a small-town greasy spoon. There was an array of food to choose from, but what I grew to love was poutine—a French Canadian dish of french fries and gravy, smothered with cheese. No doubt, it's one of the most fattening things on earth. After two months of poutine, I'd grown another thirty pounds.

So there I was, 240 pounds, still pregnant, and still very proud. Everyone was proud. Weight wasn't an issue. "Don't worry," they'd say, "you're pregnant. The weight will come off." Who was worried?

Little did they know, I was eating my poutine in private, slowly but surely becoming addicted. But this wasn't the only thing I was keeping from them. I was keeping my misery out of sight. I was eighteen years old, I had given up school to get married, and I was about to become a mother. I was petrified. And the more I ate, the more I hid my pain.

Unfortunately, my husband had no problem showing his feelings. Eventually, he started to talk about my size. "I hope you're going to lose that weight as soon as you have the baby." Well, I don't know anyone who loses one hundred pounds giving birth to a child; however, that didn't stop me from hoping, too.

His ever-growing outspokenness about my weight was becoming harder and harder to take. I was no longer his wife, the mother of his unborn child—possibly the boy he'd always wanted. I was now an overweight person who shamed him. My job, as he saw it, was to hurry up and have this baby and get back to the important things in life; namely, to lose weight and become the thinner woman he had married.

I could see this road ahead of me, and I wanted to hold on to that baby for another two years. I was smart enough and perceptive enough to know the route it was going, but I had no idea how to handle it. I would be scorned and lectured until the day I was thin. My road was mapped.

On August 18, 1975, I had my baby, Philip. He was seven pounds, thirteen ounces—a far cry from the hundred pounds I had to drop.

That first day, the family rejoiced. My father-in-law was so overwhelmed, he came to see his grandson and forgot to visit me.

My husband was also at the hospital. He told me how beautiful our son was. He also asked, "Okay, how much weight did you lose?" The question came within the first three sentences, and at that moment I knew I was in trouble.

I knew I was in trouble when he told me he was going to drive a friend to the airport, instead of taking us home from the hospital. Philip and I could take a cab.

I knew I was in trouble when I asked him to bring me a dress and he replied, "Why don't you just wear the gown home? You're too fat for your clothes anyway."

The clincher to our first family gathering was, "We're not having any friends over to see the baby until you've lost some of that weight."

I had contracted toxemia in the last few months of my pregnancy and was hospitalized. Because of the complications, the doctors had induced my labour. To me, it was a miracle my son had been born without further complications. I had delivered a strong, healthy boy, but I wasn't getting any praise for that. My pregnancy had begun with such tremendous feelings of pride, and ended with such a sense of unimportance.

Back at home, I struggled to lose a few pounds, but by this time food had become one of the few things I could hide behind and find comfort in.

To make matters more difficult, I had also become a cook at the family restaurant. It was impossible to keep my nose out of the kitchen when I was making macaroni and cheese and potato salad for five hundred people. And, of course, there was my poutine. I was around mounds of food, and I found it amusing that people thought I wouldn't eat. I was always in the kitchen—I lived there for a year and a half. I cooked and I got bigger. I made food for others and I stole some for me. I never had time to sit down for meals, so I had one continuous meal.

Just before my son's second birthday, my husband sold the restaurant. We were moving south to the big city, Toronto.

I swore I was leaving my old life behind. The Food Emporium was going to disappear in the rear-view mirror. I was on my way to a brand new condominium, where I would keep nothing but lettuce, celery and carrots in the fridge. It was going to be a new life and I promised I would succeed. My husband also promised things would be different.

I had a big job ahead of me. I was 320 pounds and I had a husband who was ashamed of me. He was so ashamed, he made the three-hour drive without stopping or pulling over for gas lest someone should see his wife. In fact, we didn't move to the heart of the city, we moved to the outskirts, where I could stay home and lose weight until I was acceptable enough for the world to see. He never said so, but I gathered as much.

The city was by no means the magical place I thought it would be. I was a country girl, I needed air; I was high in the sky in a condominium. I needed my family and my friends; I was alone.

Although the city was different, things really hadn't changed. I no longer worked at a restaurant, but we lived right around the corner from a Kentucky Fried Chicken — fast food was everywhere.

My husband's attitude hadn't changed either. But now he wasn't the only one who was repulsed by fat — the entire city seemed to hold the same notion. It was broadcast from every corner. Magazine covers were plastered with flat-chested models whose ribs stuck out. I would look at them in the store; I wasn't going to bring them home for my husband to see. Nonetheless, the messages came into my home anyway. The television brought them. The actresses, the heroines, the celebrities — all slim, all surreal.

It was unimaginable to me. This wasn't the way people behaved in the country. In the city, people were praised and admired because of their thinness, their angular bodies and their sharp jaw lines. It was so implausible that they were valued for something so vain, so vacant. I didn't understand.

I'd take my son to the playground and hear other mothers discussing how much weight they had to lose. I'd listen to the commercials that said, "lose weight and find love," or "lose weight and keep love." This I could understand. There were also messages that said "lose weight and live forever." This was a real issue; I had a son.

The one thing I knew about dieting was counting calories, counting grams, counting food. I had learned this at a diet group in the country called TOPS (Take Off Pounds Sensibly). Every meeting began with a weigh-in. If you had lost weight, everyone would applaud. If you hadn't, they would put a pig nose on you and oink. I stopped going the day they put the pig nose on me.

It doesn't take long to realize there's a sadistic sense of humour in dieting. I'd noticed that beside every Weight Watchers or diet group location, there was always a Baskin-Robbins or a Cookie Connection. I caught on to these types of barbarous tactics early in life—the amphetamines, the urine injections, and the array of unseemly operations that were made available, like stomach stapling and jaw wiring.

I remember being appalled, but at the same time laughing, "I'm going to continue this game, because everyone wants me to. But this is horrible." I was disgusted that women would go to such measures to be what others deemed acceptable. But I could empathize.

I could understand how it was possible to be brainwashed into believing that society was right. My husband had continued to be verbally abusive, and within months of moving he became physically abusive. My physician, a well-educated, seemingly caring individual, also harped on the same issues. It was as if they were part of some kind of conspiracy that had joined efforts with the diet industry. It didn't take long before I was hauling around more guilt than weight.

I couldn't remember the last time I sat down to a meal without counting the calories per tablespoon. I was so aware of everything I put in my mouth. So, if I ate a chocolate bar, I would eat in one gulp. If I didn't see it, the calories didn't count.

I spent the days wondering if I deserved to eat. How many calories had I burnt up vacuuming, walking around the park, walking around the living-room? The sound of candy wrappers became unbearably loud and oppressive. Food wasn't pleasurable anymore. So, I stopped eating.

I went on a starvation diet. After three weeks, I started to feel sick. There were dark circles under my eyes, and my nerves were raw. But I lost twenty pounds.

At least, I think I lost twenty pounds. It was hard to tell. At my heaviest I might have been 320 pounds, but our bathroom scale only went up to 300. The only way I could tell if my weight was fluctuating was by the way my underwear fit. After three weeks of eating nothing, the bathroom scale showed 298. Somehow that was a triumph in itself—being able to weigh myself.

Nonetheless, eating nothing was not the answer. Besides, I was getting angry. There were so many things I hadn't eaten. So, I binged. And, out of spite, I ate everything I had missed. By the time I finished, I was angry at eating, but mostly angry at myself.

I had succeeded by starving myself and losing weight and now—in a very mad and muddled world—I was a failure and out of control because I was putting food in my mouth.

To compensate, I combined the two. I began to binge and purge. It seemed like a perfect solution. After three months, the scale read 190 pounds. I wasn't keeping anything down, and I was losing about forty pounds a month.

In my husband's eyes, I was a success. Not surprisingly, I didn't feel like one. A voice in my head kept saying, "You poor thing."

At this point, I began to wonder what the hell I was doing. I had to get a hold of myself. Starving and bingeing. Bingeing and purging. I had to eat something, and I had to keep it down.

Somewhere I'd read about a grapefruit diet. It was just that, a diet of nothing but grapefruit. First of all, I hate grapefruit; secondly, the diet made me feel wretched. To make matters worse, I gained ten pounds in two days.

I looked for something else. But by this time, I was attending university, and all the diet books I scanned required meticulous preparation, for which I had neither the time nor the energy. What's more, going to university had given me a new perspective on things. It was another world, where people weren't obsessed about the way they looked, but about the way they felt and the way they thought. They had goals. I had been sheltered for so long, I'd forgotten this existed.

I started to feel the way I had in high school. Once again, my weight wasn't an important subject. I wanted to pursue my goals in psychology.

My husband noticed the change. His wife was enjoying her education and herself; his wife was back up to 250 pounds. Soon, he was back to his old tricks, too. The verbal and physical abuse returned.

As a result, I looked for another answer and decided on a water diet. I kept my nose in my books, and tried to keep my family life happy by spending as much time as possible with my son. I thought I would keep my husband happy by losing weight. If no food passed my lips, he would be wonderful and life would be peaceful.

Within six months I had lost more than a hundred pounds. The abuse stopped. I was pretty, but still not pretty enough. I was 140 pounds, but according to plan there was still more to go.

Once again, the little voice inside spoke. I thought I was thin enough. I was sick. I was gagging and throwing up water, my menstrual cycle was off, I was dizzy, I couldn't concentrate on my studies, my grades were slipping and my hair was falling out.

And, once again, I ate out of spite. But rather than being angry at myself, this time I was angry at anyone who had complimented me on my weight loss. I bit into each kind word with every chocolate bar and potato chip. By the time I hit 220 pounds, I was more or less satisfied with my revenge.

It was about this time my husband sat me down for a talk.

"You're so beautiful when you're thin," he said.

"You sound like an old, scratched record. I'm so tired of this. We have a problem," I said.

He nodded his head.

"We have a *marital* problem," I insisted.

"Honey, we don't have a marital problem. It's you. Look at how thin I am. I'm happy. When I go out, people don't stare at me. When I'm with you and someone snickers, it breaks my heart."

"No, it doesn't," I shot back. "It doesn't break your heart that they hurt me. *You* hurt me. It embarrasses you. You're telling me to lose weight so you can be proud. So you can look at me, and others can look at me, and think I'm beautiful."

He never got the point. He wanted us to try one more time.

He told me about a clinic he'd heard of, and he wanted to take me there. I didn't really hear much of what he said about the clinic. The only thing that stuck in my head was that *he wanted to take me somewhere*. He never took me anywhere. He was going to drive me around in broad daylight. He promised to drop me off and pick me up and look after the baby every day. I thought this was an event in itself.

Actually, I was bewildered and tired. My doctor had told me that the only other weight-loss measures left to try were having my stomach stapled or my jaws wired shut. This clinic seemed like a better alternative.

After the first visit, my husband asked how much I weighed. I told him I weighed 220 pounds. Two hundred and eighty pounds was the correct answer, but I wasn't going to admit it to him.

At the clinic I met another client. I didn't know what she weighed, but I guessed it was close to 500 pounds. We had the same weigh schedule, and saw each other every day in the waiting room. We'd make small talk to pass the time.

Lo and behold, within a few weeks my husband stopped driving me to the clinic, as I expected. So, I had a neighbour watch the baby, and I walked to my appointments.

I kept going because it was working. I stuck to my five-hundred-calorie-a-day diet of powdered shakes, and within a few months I was 220 pounds. I continued because I had already tried a million different methods, and I knew that stapling or wiring was a last resort. This clinic was my last hope.

I also kept going because leaving Philip with the neighbour gave me a chance to talk to that woman in the waiting room. Every time I went she was there. Her name was Darlene. She was a wonderful woman. And, in time, we found we had a lot in common.

She may have had more to lose, but I realized it didn't matter if she had two hundred pounds to shed and I had fifty, or vice versa, we were both the same. There were people who didn't like us for what we were. We weren't good enough. And we were both in the same place, succumbing to the same demands. Our weight difference wasn't an issue. She was feeling what I was feeling, and we instantly became friends.

After one of our daily weigh-ins, we decided to go for a doughnut and coffee. We were so guilt-ridden sitting in that coffee shop. "How does it taste?" I asked her. "Oh my God," she sighed, "I'm going to savour every bite so I can remember it." It was refreshing to eat with someone who felt the same way. She agreed. She thought it was a relief not to have her husband looking over her shoulder while she ate.

I knew exactly how she felt. Before I went on a powdered-food diet, my husband had counted the cherry tomatoes in my salad. If there were more than three, I got punched. He chained the refrigerator. These were realities in both of our lives.

It didn't take long for me to grow up. I learned so much from her. She would talk about her life—the hurdles she had to overcome and the insecurities that overwhelmed her. She told me how she felt about people not liking her, not seeing the real her, not realizing that there was an external and an internal. It may sound bizarre, but I believe we were the first people to see each other for who we really were.

So, our visits to the coffee shop became a weekly ritual. We were both on the same hamster wheel, the same path that someone else had carved out for us. It was a suffocating, restricting path. And once a week we got off of it. I can remember us standing at the counter, considering the different varieties of doughnuts. Our one chance a week to binge. Would it be cherry-filled or banana? Or how about caramel-covered? Even if the truck drivers and the housewives in the coffee shop watched us, we didn't care. We had each other.

At that time there was no group that discussed what we talked about. There were groups of fat people who got together and talked about losing weight, the trials and pitfalls of dieting, and diets themselves. But there wasn't a group where you could stand up and say, "Hey, I'm beautiful. Why can't I talk about me? Why can't I be who I am? Why can't people look inside me?" There wasn't any group where you could talk that way. So, we were a group—Darlene and I.

One day, as always, we were at the clinic. Both of us had weighed in and we'd both lost weight. We were thrilled —all the more so considering it was also our doughnut day. Outside the office, however, I realized I'd forgotten to get my week's allotment of powdered shakes. She'd wait for me in the lobby, while I went back for them.

When I got to the lobby fifteen minutes later, there was mass confusion. I started looking for Darlene—then I found her, unconscious on the floor. I was frantic, shouting at people to find out what had happened. It was just then the ambulance attendants arrived.

"I need another guy. It's a big one," one of them yelled. I remember thinking, "God, even as she's lying here, she's being insulted."

I held her hand, trying to get her to respond. I was asked by one of the attendants if I was family. No, I answered, I was a friend.

"Where's her family?" he asked.

"I don't know."

"What's her name?"

"Darlene."

"What's her last name?"

I shook my head. I never knew her last name. Somehow, I felt as if I had failed her.

As they took her into the ambulance, I saw them pull the blanket over her face.

I wondered if anybody really knew who Darlene was. Nobody saw that beautiful person, because she wasn't able to reveal the truth. She couldn't talk about her feelings, her desires or her needs — except to a person whose last name she didn't know.

Although we hadn't told each other our married names, we shared something far more significant. We shared a sense of life. It was a sense of being wanted and cared for, and having someone there to give you a hand, a hug or a peck on the cheek. We shared a fondness for each other's shortcomings, and we shared an ability to see through each other's skin.

I miss her to this day. So many times I've wished she was here to share the lessons and the laughter. But then, in a way, I know she is.

Maybe it was shock, or maybe it was whimsy, but at that very moment I decided Darlene had been a gift from God. She was an angel who had been sent to me — angels never have last names.

I sat down that night, pen in hand, and literally wrote my heart out. I finally understood calories didn't count. Those feelings about what was important in life — the ones I kept deep in my soul, the ones Darlene and I had discussed — were real and true.

And I knew I had to prove it for Darlene. I was going to start speaking up, even yelling out loud. I knew it wasn't going to be easy. It's never easy to stand up and admit you're different. But my eyes had suddenly been opened to the fact that life was about self-respect, and here and now.

My life turned 180 degrees. I no longer have to hide my fears and feelings in food. I share my needs, desires and wants more openly than I ever did. And because of this, food is no longer the most important thing in my life. I found power and grace in living for today. It makes me feel less likely to take things for granted. I'm more productive and aware. I learned that from Darlene.

Tomorrow is not an issue, nor is it a guarantee. At first, this seemed like a dangerous way of thinking. Living one day, one hour, at a time offers a solution, a way to take control of your life and change it. For a very long time, I hadn't known I had the power to make a difference.

I still have some scars from that part of my life, but I suppose what I did was a well-intentioned mistake. I was trying to fix something and I used dieting as a tool. Yes, I was out of control with food. And, yes, there were times when I ate twelve chocolate bars without coming up for air. But dieting wasn't the answer. I had so many other things hidden under that agenda that needed repair; I was using the wrong tool for the right reason.

I still have the same goals—love, self-control, beauty, happiness and success—but now I choose to seek them out directly, instead of through fluctuations in my body weight.

I chose a healthy, well-balanced lifestyle, which has nothing to do with diets. Never again will I submit my

Me and Princess.

Giving my brother, Dean, a few modelling tips.

My original home sweet home.

LYLE MCINTYRE

The headline reads "Glory of a former beast of burden." At left, me; in the middle, my sister Dale.

Philip, my little miracle of life.

PETER VIRGILE

A photo Peter took; the one that started my modelling career.

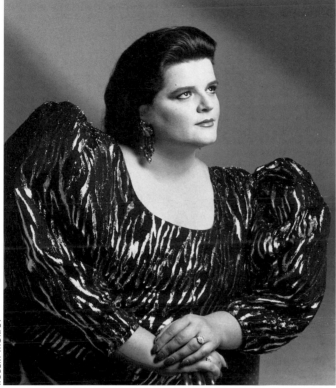

A ray of
Hope:
One of the
first plus-
size models.

ROBERT MORFEY

CRAIG SAMUEL/ORBIT

Plus Figure Models:
talent with a little extra.

CRAIG SAMUEL/ORBIT

This is what the fashion industry did to me...

This is what I did to the fashion industry.

Always there at my side, Peter.

My wedding. (Clockwise from top left: my brother Dean, Philip, my sister Dale, bridegroom Peter, sister Georgina, brother John, my father John Sr., the bride, and my mother Ruth.)

Peter and his "Bahama Mama" tanned and tuckered after a day on the beach.

Peter and Philip: the men in my life.

$1.00 U

Fall For T
Fabulous

Size 14 to 28+

Introducing Lingerie

BIG, BOLD & BEAUTIFUL BOUTIQUE
619 Yonge St., Upper Level, Toronto, Ont. M4Y 1Z5 (416) 923-4673
New address as of Oct. 1/92
1263 Bay St., Toronto, Ont. M5R 2C1 (416) 923-4673
2 Blocks North of Bloor

Big, Beautiful Brides

The Swing's the Thing

When the
weather
outside
gets frightful,
take blissful,
beautiful, cover in our
exclusive Updated Swing
Coat. We've gone to great
lengths — the latest 3/4
look — to combine warm
and wonderful in 100%
wool with cachet lining. And,
we've made it roomy enough
to wear over everything — so
roomy, in fact, that our single
size fits everyone. Styled to be
a contemporary classic with
single-button crossover closure, roll-back cuff sleeves, side
pockets and stand up collar to ward off chilling winds.
Featured is our exclusive angora-look wool melton in
richly-muted taupey tones to complement whatever you're
wearing. It's also available in solid black melton as shown.
CA06 ..... $288.00 U.S.

BB&B fashion: style that works big time.

Boldly broadcasting: Big, Bold & Beautiful's commercial.

Being coached into
fitness by Keith.

body to the stresses of yo-yo dieting. That syndrome was once the story of my life, and it left my self-esteem in tatters. In fact, I realized it was possible that I had abused my body more than my ex-husband had.

I inflicted pain on myself to make someone else happy, when all along my body wasn't the problem. Nonetheless, I thought I could fix it all with food control. But it wasn't food control—it was food elimination.

I eat more fruits and vegetables now. And I do so just because I have the choice. I've found I feel better when I eat whole-grain foods, and I'm more alert when I avoid sugary, high-fat meals. I've also found that I eat precisely when my body feels hungry. Although I was diagnosed recently as a diabetic, I've adopted these habits for the simple reason that they seem natural. Unlike dieting, these measures make sense to me.

Now I give myself the choice, because being told what to do never works. The most probable outcome is always rebellion. And, this is why the diet industry makes a fortune.

Their programs work on the very basis that you will feel successful for losing weight, and blame yourself if you don't. The diet program is never at fault. No one ever thinks that the problem lies in the very food they make you eat or the program to which you're expected to succumb. And this is why they take money from our chubby little fists and they laugh. They know people are gullible, and they're certain that we'll spend money on our dreams. They prey on our insecurities, and they dole out unrealistic diets and strategies that they say are dependent on the strength of our will-power. But they are the ones who need to exercise control. They are the ones who have to stop.

When I finally realized all these things, I found peace with dieting and my body. And, once more, food became an insignificant part of my life. It was simply a necessity. My motto had once been, "To keep my husband I have to be thin." It was now, "To keep my sanity I have to lose my husband."

I became the most important person in my life. My son was a tremendous priority, but if I wasn't healthy and happy, he wouldn't be either. I had to treat myself with importance. I had to take control of my life.

Once again, I was a young mother and I was scared to death. But, this time, I knew I would survive. There were many nights I fell asleep with my university books across my chest and my son on my stomach. We hadn't eaten much for dinner, because we didn't have much money, but it was okay. I was free.

I got rid of my crutches and I walked.

SIX

Putting Life in Motion

FOR THE LONGEST TIME, I told myself I exercised. Once in a while, when the urge struck, I would take a stroll around the block. I suppose it was exercise, but there wasn't a terrific amount of exertion involved. I certainly wouldn't boast about this physical activity, what there was of it, because secretly I was embarrassed. Even though I was getting out and stretching my legs occasionally, I had this feeling I was cheating myself.

I had so many good intentions. Actually, I had a pool of them, but I never managed to make even the slightest ripple. The pool seemed full of excuses—maybes, should haves, wannabes, can'ts. There I sat as the days passed, while this pool turned into a wishing well. There were so many things I wanted to change, but I just hung around poolside waiting for a miracle.

I kept hoping something would come my way, or someone would knock on my door with a miracle pill. Maybe they would invent something that would give me

energy, or at least motivation. There wasn't a day that
went by that I didn't dream; still, that Monday when
everything would change never came.

After years of waiting, I gave up hoping for a miracle.
I knew there had to be something to the old adage,
"God helps those who help themselves." I woke up to
the fact that if I was lucky enough to be granted a miracle or a wish, it would be far more sensible to direct it
toward something I was unable to do for myself.

It may sound corny, but I began to think I was already
pretty lucky. I had been given the gift of life. I had a
brain and a body, and if I took care of these gifts they
would last me somewhere between seventy and ninety
years.

Admittedly, I didn't adopt this philosophy whole-
heartedly at first. At the time these thoughts started to
trickle through my head, I wasn't feeling entirely lucky.
I was tired, I was out of shape, and my physical condi-
tion was suffering.

I knew I didn't look like the neighbour and I didn't
resemble anyone on a magazine cover; nonetheless, I
knew I was fortunate. I had the required allotment of
fingers, toes, legs and arms. I could walk, I could breathe,
and I was relatively healthy. It was obvious I was alive,
and from everything I had learned in the past, it was also
apparent that I had the power to change my life.

Every moment brought the opportunity to seize control of the situation. And those opportunities would be
there every day until I died, or was too sick to care. If I
wasn't happy with my body and my health, I could make
alterations. It was that simple.

Undoubtedly, physical dissatisfaction is a common
complaint among plus-size women. Feelings range from

mild irritation to full-blown anger and self-loathing. However, I had already come to accept my size; it was my shape I was dissatisfied with. Weight loss was not my goal, good health was. I knew that everyone who found out about my exercise program would assume that I was doing it to shed a few dress sizes, but that was not the case. I wanted to exercise because I wanted to keep on living.

And part of living is eating. My social activities revolve around restaurants. My friends and I are constantly exploring new culinary treats, and we do this at least three times a week. We meet and we talk, and we eat and we talk. If I wanted to maintain this social calendar, something had to be done or I'd end up at seven hundred pounds. I had to do something, and I had to get moving.

My body was becoming an obstacle in my lifestyle. It was the basis for many excuses: "I'll have to pass on that Sunday stroll [I just can't walk that far]," "You'll have to find another shortstop [Baseball? You've got to be kidding?!]" "Wish I could join you on that ski trip [I'd die before I got to the bottom of the hill]."

My body was in obvious need of repair. If it was a machine, as all the science journals claimed it was, maybe it was time to view it in the same way a proud car owner regards a classic automobile. It had been good to me. In fact, it had repaired itself in many instances during times of illness. But this body would need a little work if it was to carry me through a few more years. Basically, it needed a tune up. I didn't want my body to become irreparable.

If I was going to mend it—to follow the analogy—I'd need a tool kit. But before I could pull together the tools needed to get in shape, I had to have a plan. Sure, I could have just dropped to the floor and started right in on a few sit-ups, but this was not the time for rash moves. I had to pinpoint what needed to be fixed first.

So, like anyone who does repairs, I started with an appraisal. I stripped and evaluated myself head-on, completely naked in front of the mirror. To begin with, I made a mental list of all my positive features. I liked my breasts, my hips, my thighs, even my elbows. I took note of the smallest details, like my collar-bones, my hair and my dimples, because I knew I couldn't alter everything about myself. More to the point, I didn't want to. I had to accept my own sincere compliments before I could accept what I wanted to change.

After applauding all the wonders of my body, the negative aspects didn't seem so prominent. I simply jotted down a realistic inventory of what needed improvement. I wanted to change my belly, my upper arms and my inner thighs. It was a short list, but I knew it would be a project. It wasn't going to happen overnight.

Apart from writing down a realistic list, I also tried to adopt a realistic attitude. I was well aware these changes would take at least a year to realize, and I committed myself to twelve months of effort.

I focused on fact, not fiction. I knew there wouldn't be a 36-24-36 change. That was not what I was aiming for. Granted, I was hoping for an improvement in physical appearance, but more than that, I wanted an inner sense of well-being. I longed to be able to climb a flight of stairs without panting for air; I wanted to zip through the afternoons without dying for a nap; and I couldn't wait for the night I actually made it to my bed, instead of nodding off on the couch in front of the television set.

My goals were set. I was now ready for that tool kit.

I decided to buy myself a bright, new gym bag. Bright was the operative word; I thought if it was beaming fuchsia or purple, it would exude optimism and energy. If it was high voltage, I would be, too. I checked for little compartments and secret hideaway places to put my personal things. I also ensured the bag was made well enough to last the year—after that time, I'd treat myself to another one.

I dug through the bottom of drawers and scoured closets for old tights and leotards. The ones that fit would be worn, the ones that didn't had to go. The priority here was not that the work-out clothes be trendy and flashy, but loose and comfortable.

Next on the list was footwear. It was one investment I couldn't overlook. If I planned to move in them for twelve months, it made no sense to have shoes that made my ankles and feet suffer in the name of fitness.

Obviously, this exercise program was going to be a challenge. While I'd always relished a challenge, to ensure it wasn't all toil I borrowed Peter's walkman for the tool kit. This work-out time was going to be my time, and I wanted it to be a good time. I was going to listen to uplifting music, music *I* liked. I'd always listened to everybody else's music before—my first husband's or my son's. My favourite tunes never got that much airplay. Now they would. And, so I pulled out every '80s' tape that was covered in dust—the music everyone else seemed to roll their eyes at.

I slipped a water bottle in one of the bag's pockets, and a notepad and pencil to record my progress in another, and the tool kit was complete. I was ready to get moving. I was ready to walk.

Walking seemed the best way to start an aerobic program, because my body hadn't moved consistently in many years. It was a sensible starting point. It was also the easiest.

And so I walked. Morning, afternoon or evening, whenever I could fit it in. It didn't take long before I realized that this wasn't the way to go. I'd be too busy in the morning, and the afternoon was out of the question. I'd put off exercising until the evening, but then there were times I was too tired to put my shoes on. If this kept up, I knew I'd be right back on the couch in front of the television. I needed to block off a specific time, and I needed to stick to it. I picked the evenings. I became geared to them, and eventually it became habit-forming.

I walked every Monday, Wednesday and Friday, at the same time, for a half an hour. It was a slow start, but it was consistent. And because of this, it brought a sense of completion, control and satisfaction. There was an overwhelming feeling of pleasure in setting a goal and accomplishing it, no matter how small.

After a month, I added Tuesdays and Thursdays.

I also hunted down a few exercise videos. I looked for low-impact programs—programs I could complete—and I chose those that included women of all ages and shapes in their presentations. I'd had an eyeful of exercise videos by models and starlets, now I was looking for tapes that fit into my "realistic" program. Once a week, I would pop an exercise tape into the VCR instead of walking. My program now consisted of four days of walking for a half an hour, and one day with an exercise video.

It didn't take long to notice this new movement was creeping into other aspects of my day. If I put a load of laundry in the dryer, for example, I would run up and down the stairs a couple of times to check on it.

I was starting to feel stronger and more vigourous already. I was also starting to feel proud, and I decided to reward myself. This didn't mean I sat myself down to chocolate cheesecake—I took a long bubble bath or bought some new perfume. I had treated my body well; I also wanted to treat my psyche.

One of the rewards I didn't expect, however, was sweat. I couldn't remember the last time I had perspired; it was remarkable. I knew if I was sweating, I was really working out. From then on, I anticipated the moment those little beads appeared on my forehead.

I kept my statistics and within six months I had lost fifteen pounds, I was full of energy and sleeping well. I felt wonderful and completely positive.

Then everything crashed in. Old attitudes began clouding my view. It was such a long journey. It was taking so long. I needed to remind myself of things I had said before: "Too far for what? Who are you comparing yourself to? Over who's weight?" I was prepared for these drawbacks. It was the first of a few times I had to get myself back on track.

At one point during the process, Peter remarked, "Why don't you try something different? Come to the gym and meet my personal trainer."

"What do you mean?" I said in defense. "I'm not good enough the way I am? What I'm already doing isn't good enough?"

"What you're doing is great," Peter answered cautiously. "I'm very proud of you, but I think you could get better results quicker, with the same amount of effort."

I didn't know what he was saying. "Quicker? What could happen quicker? Losing weight? Now you're not happy with the way I look?"

He stressed that he was talking about results, and if I didn't like the word "quicker," maybe "easier" would make his point clear. I still didn't understand. I thought his attitude was changing toward me. Because he was improving quickly, he wanted me to do the same. I was sure he was seeking control. I was furious with him, and I stopped exercising for two weeks.

For years I had punished my first husband by not exercising, and here I was years later punishing my new husband because I assumed he thought I wasn't getting results fast enough. Even though I missed the walks and the videos, out of rebellion I just stopped moving.

Peter never brought it up again, and he didn't remark on my abandoned exercise program.

Eventually I saw that Peter had been trying to help by pointing out exercising could be more productive (assuming that's what I wanted) if I recruited a coach.

I didn't know if I wanted a coach. I didn't know if I wanted to go to a gym. "Is the gym intimidating?" I asked. Actually, I grilled him. "Who goes there? What do they look like? Are there any big people?" He shared his experiences with me, and before long I asked him to set up a meeting with his trainer.

A week before the appointment, I began to wonder what this trainer was like. "Is he nice? What does he look like?" I thought if he was a big, blond, bronzed muscle-head I was in trouble. "What's the first thing he does in the meeting?" I wanted to know. First, I was told, he took down your statistics—your measurements, your weight. Oh, no. See my weight? Take my measurements?

Forget it. Cancel my appointment. Peter tried to reassure me that he would be there right beside me. It was a very kind offer, but it didn't stop me from feeling as if I might wet myself.

The next week came and Peter drove me to the meeting. The closer we got, the more it felt like driving to prison. Somehow, I managed to find my way through the doors and meet the trainer, Keith—he was very kind, not the sergeant-major I'd envisioned.

He explained the program he'd set up—Peter had told him all about me before I arrived, actually he warned him—and then he had me try the stationary bicycle. After five minutes I thought I would die, but five minutes was all I was supposed to do. I made it, and my self-respect surged. Not surprisingly, it was muscle pain that surged the next day.

Within three months, I was meeting with Keith three times a week as well as working out with Peter in the gym. My training sessions were held in a separate area away from the main sports club and, at most, I would be exercising with ten other people in the room. This seclusion was comfortable and safe. But, as soon as I felt completely settled in, we were informed the lease had run out on our isolated spot, and we'd have to move to the main gym.

"Are you comfortable with this?" Peter asked. I had no idea. What was this main gym everyone was warning me about? Our moving date was set for the following week, and anxiety began to set in. This wasn't exercise; this was an emotional roller-coaster ride.

One week later, I drove alone to the main gym. As I pulled up, it felt like starting all over again. I was scared. Past the doors, there was a stockpile of equipment, besieged by men. The sound was deafening—the grunt-ing, the moaning. I had left my quiet little work-out space across the way for this huge area, with huge men with huge muscles.

I turned to the receptionist and asked where the change room was and where I could find the relocated private gym. She pointed, and her finger seemed to go on forever. The change room was at the very end of the room, past the men, past the groans. From there, I'd have to walk up an open flight of stairs in full view of everyone. I could not do it. I couldn't handle the sce-nario—Big Girl Goes into Big Gym. I could see their muscles bulging; I could just imagine their eyes doing the same. I panicked and ran out of the gym.

A few blocks away, I pulled my car over and cried. Then I called Keith. "I'm sorry. I just can't do it. I just can't work out there." He empathized and told me to take a few days to think about it.

He didn't have to tell me to think about it; it was all I thought about. I felt as if I had let hundreds of people down. Here I was, a plus-size expert, spouting off on issues, trying to instill confidence among my peers and acceptance in society, and I was intimidated. It was a very human, very natural reaction, but I felt like a coward.

In two days, Keith called back. "I want you back in the gym," he said. "Look, I'll walk you through. I'll hold on to you." It took much reassurance and arm-twisting, but it worked.

I returned. Clinging to Peter on one side, and Keith on the other, I made it through the gym and up the stairs. When I was done, they escorted me back out the front door. We did that for a week.

The next week, I tried it without my training wheels. I walked alone; my heartbeat kept time. It was so uncomfortable, it was painful. But every time I conquered my fears, I felt a new satisfaction—the same satisfaction I felt when I had first completed an exercise. It became a celebration of setting my sights on something and attacking.

Today, one year later, I'm downstairs with the big boys. I realized these men—these muscle-men—are so involved in themselves and their own bodies, they don't care how you look or why you look a certain way. They're actually encouraging. All of them, women included, come over to say, "Keep it up, Jackqueline, you're doing great." They show me different methods of exercising and tricks they've learned themselves.

I know they're not looking at me; if anything, they celebrate the fact that we're all there for the same reason—to work on our bodies and to feel better. Of course, it would have been a relief to know these things at the outset. But I suppose, as it is with everything, I had to learn for myself. If nothing else, it's been an exhilarating learning experience.

Apart from learning the simple facts of the gym, I also realized my goals had changed. When you aim for something and reach it, you move on. Ambitions naturally change. When you see they're attainable, you're impelled to shoot for higher levels of performance. Marathon swimmers don't start out wanting to be marathon swimmers—they start off in a little pool surrounded by loved ones who tell them they're successful; they move on to small races and then to larger competitions; and, eventually, they become marathon swimmers.

It starts with realistic goals. I wanted to feel better and improve my heart rate—that simple. I wanted to be able to climb a flight of stairs. I wanted to be able to continue a work-out program on a regular basis without fleeing for the couch. It may sound simple, but in the beginning it was very difficult.

However, once I attained those goals, my targets became more specific. I wanted to focus on a certain area and tone another. My goals were never dress sizes. They were based on performance rather than physical attributes. For example, I would attempt the Stairmaster for fifteen minutes at level four, and the next week I would work up to twenty minutes at level five. These pay-offs were much more of a challenge. I was able to set them and I was able to reach them. They were realistic and they never focused on my body image.

In fact, my original goal of being able to continue an exercise program seemed to vanish. Exercising has become a natural part of my week. I've enjoyed the experience so much, it's become a part of my life. Granted, I still enjoy not working out on the days I have free, simply because I've given myself permission not to exercise. And I make sure exercising doesn't become mundane by finding different methods and machines. In all, I've found I'm now able to move my body in ways I never could before.

Apart from the sweat, the flexibility, the energy and the confidence moving my body has brought me, one of the greatest achievements came recently when—of all things—I had a gall-bladder operation.

I was back in the gym seven days after I was released from the hospital. Of course, I took it very slowly and gently, nonetheless people were amazed. Even my physician said people at my weight generally take four weeks to recover from such major surgery.

But, the most exhilarating reward came soon after I awoke from the operation. The head surgeon had stopped by to check on me. He was reading my chart, prodding and poking. Then he said, "It might be too personal, but I'd like to ask you something." Well, this man had seen me buck naked, upside down on an operating table, where gravity isn't very kind. What could possibly be more personal than that?

"Do you exercise?" he asked.

I was taken aback; it wasn't what I had expected. "Why?"

"Well," he explained, "I must say you're in excellent shape."

I was shocked.

"All through the operation," he continued, "we were talking about you."

They were talking about me when I had no clothes on?

"In fact," he said, "we were taking bets as to whether you exercised."

"What would give you reason to do that?" I asked.

"During the height of the operation, your resting heart rate was sixty-five. Normally, someone your size would have a heart rate of more than ninety-five. I just had to ask."

It certainly was an unusual question. Yet, he had seen the body of someone who may not have exercised and, at the same time, the heart of someone who could. I looked at him and said, "I do work out."

"Keep up the good work," he grinned. "It shows."

That surgeon not only gave me the best compliment I could ever imagine, he confirmed something I'd always believed: it's not the body's image that matters, but the heart that's beating inside.

SEVEN

Uncovering the Sensual Woman

WELL, ALL THOSE JOKES about the farmer's daughter
are not true. The sordid details you hear about the
haystack and the travelling salesmen do not exist. Not in
my case, at any rate. I was a country girl without a sexual life.

I was incredibly naive about sex. Sure, like everyone
else, I first kissed a boy at the age of ten, but that's as
far as it, or I, went.

I was a virgin bride at eighteen, and my son was born
a year later. The chance to explore sexual activity was
rare at best.

During my pregnancy, my husband's verbal displea-
sure of my ever-growing body became all the more fre-
quent. Those opinions lasted throughout our marriage.
All he ever wanted was the young woman he had orig-
inally married.

Consequently, I only exposed my body in the dark,
under the covers. I never had sex during daylight or with

the lights on, because my body would be in full view of his critical eyes. I knew he thought my flesh was repulsive, and I didn't want to repulse him. His comfort had been my comfort, and I did anything to soothe the situation. Stroking my large belly or caressing my thighs was not acceptable. It would only contribute to my sense of shame and furtiveness. So, I didn't make them available to him. I had sex in the missionary position, never experimenting or instigating new and different possibilities.

He didn't seem to understand that criticism was not a form of foreplay. He honestly believed if I lost weight, I would become the sexual woman he wanted me to be. In his mind, having a body both of us could be proud of was the missing aphrodisiac.

We developed an angry and resentful intimate relationship. I accused him of being controlling and manipulative; he blamed me for being self-conscious, ashamed and passionless. Unfortunately, and tragically, we were both right.

I avoided sex for years. On the rare occasions when I did crawl under the covers with my husband, it was only out of wifely duty. It made him happy. It stopped the arguing.

We constantly fought about sex. We battled over its lack of frequency, its lack of sincerity, and the lack of any form of affection. Still, I couldn't find it in my heart to let him love me with the very hands that abused me.

I ended the relationship for this and many other reasons. However, they all culminated into one forceful effect—I didn't feel like an attractive, wanted woman. On the contrary, I felt miserably ugly and unfit. When I left my husband, I knew that one of the greatest tasks ahead of me would be to uncover my sensual side.

For years, the belief that I wasn't an attractive and sensual woman imprisoned me in dowdy bras, full-cut polyester underwear and flannel nightgowns. At the time, it seemed justified: I deserved to be hidden. The very man who had told me he loved me, who had had a son with me, couldn't be bothered to look at me. Why should I or anyone else? My first husband had considered my body an eyesore—one that must be concealed by baggy and lifeless undergarments.

Comments like, "You have such a pretty face" didn't help. I knew the rest of the sentence went, "What happened to the rest of you?" even if the words were never spoken. These remarks didn't boost my self-esteem, they made me want to hide all the more.

For years, I had a relationship with my own form from the neck up. My body from the neck down didn't exist. I would wash my face in the morning, comb my hair, brush my teeth, and forget about the rest. I didn't see it in the bathroom mirror; it didn't matter. It carried me from place to place, but we weren't in unison, my body and I. I only existed in my head. I managed to erase everything else.

However, this relationship couldn't continue either. I couldn't go on ignoring my body forever. I wanted to embrace it, I wanted to love it, but I didn't know how—and I didn't know if I should.

I knew there were millions of people on the planet who had sexual lives. They had sensual lives. They loved their bodies and their bodies were in motion. My body was just lying there, ready to decay. It wasn't living, it was existing. It was a frightening realization.

I presumed that building self-esteem included establishing a sexual identity. And I gathered that this would also involve having a sexual relationship with someone who could accept my body the way it was. But I wasn't going to be frivolous with relationships—there would be no one-night stands. At that particular time, I didn't think I could get a one-night stand, but if it was available to me I wasn't going to participate in that sort of activity. I didn't want to cheapen myself just to satisfy my overwhelming desire to be held, stroked, loved and appreciated.

I had to figure it out for myself first. I wanted to love myself before I looked for a sexual partner. It might have been easier to look for love on the outside, but I knew I would probably end up back in the same situation. I would set myself up to be loved, cared for and then abused because I wasn't what they wanted. I wasn't prepared to be thrown away again.

I had to rebuild myself by myself. The only person who could afford the time and energy to repair Jackqueline was Jackqueline.

I began by telling myself every day that I loved who I was, the way I was. I would look in the mirror and repeat over and over, "I'm a good person, with a strong, wonderful body."

Negative programming from the past made it horribly difficult to believe this at first. Every once in a while, a comment someone had made would surface in my head and haunt me. "How can I love me, and think so highly of myself, if people think so little of me?" Still, I kept reaffirming the fact that I was beautiful.

I focused on positive aspects, rather than negative ones. "You have such a lovely smile/gorgeous hair/delicate shoulders/cute kneecaps." I looked for anything and everything likeable about myself to confirm there was reason to be proud.

I desperately tried to attach buts. "But my breasts sag." "But my belly's big." "But my thighs are huge." For every affirmation, there was an insult ready to be hurled back at the reflection in the mirror. It was a struggle to hold back those negative comments. They were there on a subconscious level, but only the positive comments passed my lips.

Looking in the mirror itself was quite a startling experience. Of course, I used this trick years later when I was ready to start exercising, but this was the first time in a long time I had faced myself head-on. Near the end of my first marriage, the mirror had simply been a place where I fixed the part in my hair or flossed my teeth; now I was standing in front of it naked. It was astonishing, but I continued to do it. I've always believed in the saying, "Fake it, until you make it." So I kept telling myself I was beautiful, over and over, forgetting my "buts."

As the weeks and months passed, I began to find wonderful things in the mirror. Then, one fateful day, something miraculous happened. There in the mirror was a faint image of a blossoming woman. I finally saw her. And I realized no one had the right to say she wasn't beautiful.

If beauty was in the eye of the beholder, then what I was beholding was truly beautiful. I was the only one looking, and I wasn't judging. That was the key. I had come in contact with myself first. I was that one-and-only beholder and I found true inner and outer beauty. It certainly wasn't vanity, it was simply realizing that everyone deserves to like and appreciate themselves for their real worth.

I was physically the same size when I found myself looking back from the reflection, but there was a radiance, a warmth and a gleaming from my eyes. I looked completely different. It was a breath of fresh air. It was another turning point.

I started to appreciate the new found me. I bought perfume to spray on my voluptuousness, I grew my hair longer in order to frame my lovely, ample body and I bought naughty, delicious underwear. There were long robes, silk teddies, bustiers and push-up bras, satin thongs, thigh-highs and silk stockings.

With these, I discovered a new sense of myself. I selfishly wore them, without excuses, for my own pleasure. And, it came as an unexpected pleasure to know I could wear them just for me, and no one else. These sexy, luxurious things against my skin became my sweet secret.

One night I was feeling romantic. However, I was alone. I dressed in a bustier, garters and silk stockings. I danced to soft music by soft candlelight. I'll never forget that night. It was the first time I discovered sensuality. My body and my soul seemed to be in unison as they slowly danced together.

The experience reminded me of watching a film in reverse. My whole life seemed that way. I was the Humpty Dumpty who had to piece herself back together. It wasn't as if no one else knew how to, but I wanted the luxury of doing it myself. And it *was* a luxury. I was doing it the way I wanted it done, the way I dreamed and fantasized a sensual, sexy woman should be. I didn't want to be the replica of someone else's fantasy or desires.

I needed to find out who this twenty-four-year-old woman was, but I wanted to keep it a secret until I was ready to reveal her to the world. Not that the rest of the world mattered, but I knew I couldn't live in isolation forever. More importantly, I understood that I needed to be entirely acquainted with myself before I could reflect that to the world. Then it would be easier to find someone who would fall in love with that true reflection. It was all the more worthwhile knowing I was already in love with the familiar reflection of myself in the mirror.

I have memories of one particular day when I cleaned my house in the nude. I remember how freeing it was; I also recall a definite sense of guilt. It was a constant battle of progression and regression. I didn't feel entirely natural being "au naturel," but I needed to, more so I wanted to.

Eventually I did. One evening, again alone, I did a slow striptease to Rod Stewart's "Do You Think I'm Sexy?" The music was sultry and so was I.

Because of this new sense of sensuality, family and friends began commenting on my appearance. They would say, "You look like you've lost weight." Of course, I hadn't lost any weight; what they were really seeing was this new sense of self. I was, in fact, a sensual, living being. I had developed stature and presence. I had undergone a slow metamorphosis, becoming comfortable with myself and loving myself. But there was still a residue of my vulnerability. I started experiencing a disturbing and confusing split between seeing myself as beautiful and as undesirable, particularly when I started getting attention from men.

I was severely frightened. I was convinced I should act as though I never expected any decent, normal man to look at me sexually. Yet, at the same time, I felt ashamed that I was displaying my sexuality for all the world to see.

I felt as if I was on centre stage with strobe lights highlighting my body. All the familiar fears of abuse and rejection filled my head and restrained my heart. I withdrew into my cocoon and returned to my faithful companion, food.

Suddenly, I didn't have any privacy or secrecy. I had learned to accept myself, but would they? I was so afraid of scorn. I certainly didn't have any right to assume that any man would want me. How disgusting and pathetic for me to even remotely believe in those possibilities.

Ashamed, I buried all of my risqué underwear in the bottom drawer. I eliminated the pleasure of self-acceptance. I suppressed my joy and laughter. I stopped smiling at men, and I stopped smiling at my reflection in the mirror.

It had all been too close for comfort. Consequently, I defined any further sexual interest expressed toward me as perverse. Any man who expressed interest in me was disturbed and just had the hots for obese women.

After a few months, however, feeling unworthy of attention became unbearable. I had such high expectations of negativity, and that was scaring me more than dancing or feeling good about myself. I missed feeling wonderful and uninhibited.

So, once again, I faced the mirror. It was like starting over, but at least I knew the path. It was easier to believe the good things this time. And it was important. I didn't plan to live my life alone.

I took long bubble baths, I played soft, romantic music and I rescued my sexy underwear. Slowly, I forged ahead.

I avoided looking for perfection in the mirror. In fact, I learned no one knows what perfection is—is it three inches off the waist, two inches off the stomach, the cover of *Vogue*? It didn't exist; it didn't matter. Throughout the journey, I kept reminding myself I didn't have to strive for perfection, but just venture boldly to a land of confidence.

Then I met Peter. He became a very dear friend. And he had this wonderful habit of giving me compliments. At first, they were difficult to accept because he was so good-looking. He was hot, as a matter of fact; he was a model. And he persisted. Peter was also a sounding board for me. I was able to talk to him openly and honestly, in a way I hadn't been able to speak to anyone before. He, too, helped me realize how wonderful I was. He reaffirmed what I believed, and I realized I had been lucky to find someone who loved me for who I was and what I was—the way I loved myself.

There's an old saying I've always been fond of: As life unfolds, there are bound to be a few wrinkles. I'm glad this particular set of wrinkles has been ironed out.

I was right all along about loving myself first. Through this experience, I found beauty and a bridge to my sexuality.

As Peter and I became closer over the years, our friendship turned into something much more. We became lovers; we became husband and wife.

In our sexual relationship we have always known that humour is vital. Granted, there are moments of intense intimacy and passion, but in general we've always brought along a sense of humour and imagination. We know sex is an important aspect of a relationship, and we know it doesn't always come easily.

There's no doubt it takes imagination and effort to allow yourself to enjoy the freedom of sex. The bedroom is no place to have hang-ups about the size of your breasts, your belly or your thighs. It's not a place for inhibitions, it's a place to bare all.

And, over the years, Peter and I have done some pretty bizarre baring. We've performed stripteases, his and her, with outlandish costumes—do-it-yourself pluck-the-feathers or burst-the-balloons. We've donned pajamas we've meant to throw away and ripped them off each other. There have been Silly-String fights. We've worn headphones and listened to our separate, favourite tunes. And we've played odd and unexpected characters. Basically, it's always different.

Admittedly, this is pretty extroverted behaviour, but it isn't always like that. There are also moments of quiet, or evenings with gentle music, candles and potpourri. For each individual, and each individual moment, the ingredients of passion are unique. The essential component is having a beautiful man next to you who appreciates you and your beautiful body.

Looking back now, it seems my path to finding sensuality and sexuality was pretty clear-cut. 1) Take off your clothes in front of the mirror; 2) Have a good look at yourself and like it; 3) Buy sexy underclothes; 4) Feel proud and it will show; and 5) Find true love. It may sound like a cut-and-dry five-step program, but it wasn't. Yes, I devised these methods (and, in some cases, I simply fell over them), and yes, they were advantageous. However, they weren't clear-cut.

Because my first marriage was abusive, I didn't walk away from it feeling terrific about myself. At twenty-four, all I knew was that I needed work and I needed to be nourished. It took me two years to start putting Humpty Dumpty back together again.

Unfortunately, when you fall into the category of a Humpty Dumpty, everything breaks at once—your emotional self, your physical self, your inner strength. However, when you start putting the pieces back together, they each need individual attention. It would have been much easier if I had only needed to repair one aspect of myself, but my sexuality was just one of many fragments. To be able to move on to other parts of my life, I had to put it in place.

As it was with everything, it was a matter of two steps forward and one step back. For every dynamic advance, there was a hasty retreat. There was no use feeling badly about that step back; it was part of the progress. You learn from your mistakes.

Sure, three steps forward and no looking back is ideal—in an ideal world—but that doesn't happen. No one lives their life every day believing whole-heartedly that they're wonderful. No matter how many times I told myself how beautiful I was, there were still days when I felt like the ugliest thing on the planet. Maybe it was PMS, or maybe someone said something that upset me. I'd spent so many years in a marriage in which I was being blamed for someone else's problems, it was an automatic reaction to blame myself when things went wrong. Then I'd take that step back.

But no day is the same. I knew the whole point was to never give up. I was building something block by block, and if by chance some gale-force wind came along and knocked a few blocks off, so be it; I could rebuild. I knew I'd get to a point where there was no looking back. I had my eye on the horizon, and taking one step backward meant nothing.

I was trying to find pieces to rebuild and, in a sense, I suppose I was soul searching. I wanted to feel like a woman, not just a person. I hadn't felt any sexuality before. I had given birth to a child, but I didn't feel like a woman. I needed to come in contact not only with who I was, but what I was and what I was worth.

By coming to terms with myself, I realized I was soft and feminine. I was a woman who loved to dance and laugh. This woman I had become was just fine—she didn't need anything else.

Not too long ago, I was asked to speak on this topic on a talk show. The subject was, "People who are fat and feel sexy." Even the title had a slightly hard and tacky resonance. I was told they planned to have large ladies, dressed in bustiers, fishnet stockings and stilettos, noise off about their sexual magnetism. It sounded obnoxious. It didn't sound like my style at all.

I turned down the offer, because I didn't have, or want, to be obnoxious to prove my sexuality. I'm sexy in my own way—the way I walk, the way I talk, the way I dress. It may be obvious to some, but it is in no way painfully obvious. My individual sexuality has come from the time I have spent alone with myself, a time that allowed me to cocoon and blossom. Besides, I had this feeling that the women who would want to be on that show were not truly at peace with their womanliness. Being a woman is not something that requires exaggeration. The point to finding my sexuality was to bring it forth, not to parade it. I was prepared early on for the possibility that I may not have had any particular strong sense of sexuality. There are a lot of non-sexual people in the world; it's simply not part of their chemistry. If the same was true for me, that was fine, I could accept that.

I just wanted to know. I wanted to find out for myself. Through it, I've learned that it's fine to dance alone on a dance floor; it's all right to have sexual feelings and no one to share them with; it's right to have positive feelings; and, it's perfectly acceptable to have negative thoughts. It's okay to be yourself. Only then can you go forward.

EIGHT

The Clothes Call

MY WHOLE FAMILY, including my two brothers and two sisters, has always had a thing for clothes. When I was small, I would watch the way my older sisters dressed, and on the occasion they brought magazines home, I'd leaf through them, too.

Apart from this fascination with clothing, I also had a fascination with dolls. I started collecting them from the age of three and by the time I was eleven I had forty-five—some walked, some talked, the rest had their own particular talents. Not only did I love them, I was pre-occupied with them. I would sit for hours and do their hair, put my mother's make-up on them, change their outfits, and when they got dirty, I washed them.

One day at school, my brothers, sisters and I were called down to the principal's office. We were told there had been an electrical fire at our house, and the school bus driver would take us to our grandmother's, while they contacted our parents at work.

"Are my dollies okay?" was the first thing out of my mouth. Of course, the principal couldn't tell me. He didn't know.

On the way to grandmother's house, I kept questioning my sisters on the state of my dolls. Did they think they were all right? Did they think their clothes would be dirty?

The route to Grandma's went right past our house. I remember pressing my nose against the bus's rear window. All that was left was smoldering rubble.

I knew my dollies were nowhere in sight. It was devastating. Those dolls had been like babies to me.

We lost everything in that fire, including Princess. All that was salvaged was what had been left on the clothesline—some underwear, a few nightgowns and a couple of sheets.

For me, all that was left was on my back. I'd been wearing a navy blue jumper (I remember it like it was yesterday; it had a band around the waist and big box pleats), a little white shirt and matching knee socks. That became my outfit for the next four months. I didn't have anything else to wear, except for a nightie that had been saved from the line.

Because my parents weren't wealthy, there wasn't the money to buy new clothes for five children. They managed to pull together enough money for rent on a new home, and they managed to put food in our mouths.

Of course, the children at school teased me for wearing the same outfit day in and day out. It didn't matter that my parents kept me extraordinarily clean. In fact, cleanliness kept me from school about once a week. Our mother washed our clothes by hand, and sometimes I'd miss school because mine hadn't dried in time.

These were trying times for all of us. We lived in a one-room cabin, and we took turns sharing the bed. Every other day we'd have a whole sandwich for lunch —the days in between were half-sandwich days (which may explain my love of food).

It was during this time that I began to dream about having a closet packed with beautiful clothing. At eleven, I wasn't old enough to earn money to buy my own clothes. I had to depend on what my parents could afford. And, understandably, their priorities were keeping a roof over our heads and food in our stomachs. So I fabricated fantasies about how I would dress myself. I would lie in the grass, look up at the clouds and see Victorian dresses with bustles and bows, exotic fabrics and intricate patterns.

As I got older, I began borrowing clothes from my sisters, although "borrowing" probably isn't the right word. When one of my sisters would come home from university on the weekends, I would go through her things just before she packed to leave. I'd take out a pretty blouse or something that caught my eye. And I'd wear it until she returned the next week, when I'd put it back and take something else.

I still dreamt about fashion. One day, walking through town, I spotted an outfit in a shop window—purple gingham hotpants and a purple turtleneck to match. It was gorgeous. I'd never seen anything like it (nor have I seen anything like it since). I started visiting the window every day, just to look, because that was all I could do with this dreamy outfit. It was priced at $220, which was my parents' paycheques put together. It was ridiculous, but it was so fabulous.

I must have voiced my feelings, because my parents

bought the outfit for my birthday. I was more than over-whelmed; I couldn't believe it.

I wore those hotpants everywhere. I went to a dance at the Holiday Inn and was spotted by a photographer who asked me to model in them for the opening of a car lot. Why not? I was 5'8", 130 pounds. I was proud of myself and, God knows, I was proud of those hotpants. I ended up modelling that outfit a few times. And, in a funny way, it became an important aspect of my life.

No matter how revered those hotpants were, I still kept fantasizing about clothes. I wasn't able to sew, nor was anyone else in the family, so those dream clothes just hung in my head. To compensate, I cut out pictures from catalogues and some of my mom's magazines and started a scrapbook of different outfits I would wear if I had the money. It was never how I wanted to look phys-ically; it was just what I would buy. It was a wish book, and it was divided into sections. The titles read, "This is what I would wear in the daytime"; "This is what I would wear to the office" (although I was still in high school); "This is what I would wear in the evening"; and "This is what I would wear in the bedroom."

Thinking back now, there was an abundance of feath-ers, sequins and boas. It was all very dramatic, which is a riot considering I was such an introvert.

I carried that thing around with me. It didn't matter what I was wearing, I always felt well-dressed because I had the scrapbook. I didn't have those clothes on my back, but I had them nonetheless.

When I started working part-time, I started slowly building that wardrobe. It wasn't as extravagant or expensive, but I was developing a sense of what the scrapbook represented.

I remember going to school in a three-quarter-length, grey suede coat, black jodhpurs, knee-high black suede boots and a colourful headband. I thought I was cool (which, for some reason, was a high priority in the '70s). I had bell-bottoms, pop tops, mini skirts and everything else that was considered fashionable, but I always managed to throw them together in a particular style — my style.

I used to get compliments from people at school. They wanted to know where I got stuff and how I put it together. I had this habit of mixing things up — changing belts, adding scarves and whatnot. And because I did some modelling — the car lot, a Holiday Inn brochure and a few vacation guides — I guess they thought I was in the fashion realm (or whatever degree of fashion realm there was in a small town in the '70s).

I'd dress my sisters and my friends. We'd go into stores and spend the day trying on different outfits and basically playing dress-up. I loved it, and it made them feel good.

I must have made some impact. The week after I got married, the local paper celebrated my wedding with a full-page write-up and a photo of the bride. But, of course, after that fateful day things changed.

I began gaining weight and losing self-esteem. I started to hide behind shabby, drab clothing; I wasn't feeling secure enough anymore to wear vivid colours. I developed three new rules of fashion: a) never dress in a sexy way; b) never dress in an attractive way; and c) never dress in any way that makes you stand out in a crowd.

I lived by those rules for a long time. In fact, it got to a point where I wouldn't even wash my hair or think about putting on make-up. I concealed myself in tent dresses. For years, I walked around in bag-like garments with no shape, never acknowledging there was a body inside, or a personality for that matter. I didn't want to show the world what I was all about, so I shielded myself behind horrible clothing.

When my marriage ended, my self-confidence resurfaced. Walking along the street one day, I noticed a plus-size store. I was curious, so I went in. They had beautiful designs from all over the map. As I was browsing, I caught myself in the mirror. I saw a typical, despairing, solemn housewife who hadn't a care about her appearance — and I knew that's what the salespeople were thinking too. Not only did I look like I couldn't afford their clothes, I couldn't. I kept looking anyway. Then a woman approached me from the back of the store. She wondered if she could help, but I was just looking. So we chatted. I left the store, but ventured back the next week.

I was feeling better this time; I had fixed my hair and put on my best outfit. The same woman came over to see me. She was the owner. As I was looking, I came across a number of wonderful items. She suggested I put them on lay-away and pay them off in time. Even though my budget was excruciatingly tight, I decided to take her advice. And because she was so lovely and made me feel so welcome and wonderful, I kept going back.

One day she called to tell me she was holding a fashion show, and asked if I would be one of her amateur models. There was really no such thing as professional plus-size models at that time; she was using her clients instead. I decided to try it, and agreed to meet the choreographer, who was going to teach us how to walk.

Peter was that choreographer—it was our first meeting —and because of his encouragement and the exhilarating experience of walking down a runway, I eventually became a plus-size model.

But to be a model I needed a well-rounded wardrobe, which at the time I didn't have. It was at that time that Peter did something I'll never forget.

I had previously given Peter the keys to my apartment in case of emergency (he was always concerned for Philip's and my safety). I came home one night and, as usual, went to hang up my coat. It was worn and a bit torn. As I hung it up, I noticed another one next to it. I yelled out, "Hello," thinking someone was in the apartment. No answer. I took the coat off its hanger. It was the most beautiful trenchcoat I'd ever seen—and I'd never seen it before. A note was pinned to its label: "Jackqueline, you're beautiful. Wear it in good health. Love, Peter." I put my arms through the sleeves, and grabbed the phone to thank him. He said he wanted me to feel proud walking around to my modelling bookings, and he took a part-time job delivering flowers to make sure it happened (the job, of course, was to pay off the coat). He was a good friend and he was supportive, and that, in itself, was more than enough for me. I didn't want him to go to those lengths, but he insisted. One more reason for me to feel very special.

And so my modelling career began. I posed for catalogue pictures and department store ads, and I walked down runways.

After I'd finish a fashion show, there would be a lineup of women waiting for me outside the change room. "How did you wear that belt with that light beige suit? Who makes the blouse you wore with the suit? Who does your hair? How do you put on your make-up?" There was a barrage of questions from these women who came to the malls to see fashion shows.

It became very obvious, very fast, that there was a demand for someone in the fashion industry to take plus-size women by the hand and teach them a few tricks. It was also pretty apparent from some of the clothes I was asked to wear that there was a need for some kind of advocate who would fight with manufacturers for clothes that plus-size women wanted and needed. I knew a lot of these questioning women had exceptional taste, but they hadn't had the opportunity, or the garments, to bring it out.

It was a little different for me. Through my teenage scrapbook and my experience as a plus-size model, I'd had a chance to experiment with ideas. Obviously, being dressed for the camera in a variety of looks (ones I couldn't yet afford) and being played with by a variety of fashion stylists was a unique opportunity. But for everyone else, there was a glaring need for more opportunity, more options and, at the very least, attention.

I used to talk to Peter about it. I'd tell him about the women and their questions. These women would ask if I held imaging seminars—I didn't and I didn't know anyone who did. More to the point, I didn't know why no one did. From a business standpoint it would have been lucrative, but more importantly, there was such a tremendous necessity.

Consequently, I started to think of ways I could help women at large. I felt I had an innate responsibility to do that. Maybe, *I* could hold seminars.

I decided to start by writing down a ten-year plan (always thinking big, never thinking small). I set out to make another scrapbook. It began with a company name. Large, Lovely Lady? No. Something else. There were so many possible titles. Then I came up with Big, Bold & Beautiful. I liked it, and I wrote it down on the cover.

The next step was to find a place to teach these seminars. At the time, Peter was taking singing classes from a woman who had a small studio on Yonge Street in downtown Toronto. She only used it twice a week. I thought we might be able to use it a few nights when she wasn't. Peter thought it was a good idea, but wondered what we'd pay her with. It was a good question. I didn't have a penny and Peter couldn't help me—he was still paying off my coat.

We approached her anyway. She liked the idea too, and said she'd charge us $20 a night. She understood our meagre situation and decided we didn't have to pay her until after two weeks of use. But it was a business deal, so she asked for a $20 security deposit. It seemed fair, but all I had on me was a government baby bonus cheque—for $20. She'd take it. I signed the back and handed it over. "Okay," she said, "this is the start of your business."

We'd have the studio the next week. In the meantime, we decided to run a small ad in a local paper: "Personal-development classes for plus-size women. Self-confidence, self-esteem, make-up, hair and wardrobe. Call, 923-HOPE." It was Peter's home phone number. Calls would come in to the answering machine in his bedroom. I would sit there, in the evenings, behind a desk calling people back and setting up appointments for our introductory meetings.

I had given myself a month to sell the idea to women, before the actual workshops began. All I had to sell the concept was my little, pink modelling portfolio that held my modelling pictures.

So we made up a little brochure for the event. It outlined what I was going to teach and had my picture emblazoned on the front. Peter had typed it up, it was photocopied (we couldn't afford to have them printed), and we folded them by hand.

I had seven names in my appointment book for the first introductory meeting. Out of seven, five women showed, and I pitched them the workshops.

One of them laughed, "You're going to teach it here?!" I said we all had to start somewhere. She asked how much the course was; I asked her how much she could afford. It didn't matter; she wasn't interested. As it stood, no one was.

We had to figure out how to sell this idea. We thought we should at least clear out the room so it would look a bit bigger. We moved the music books and hid the music stands.

We decided to put a little more information about the course on the brochure and, this time, we included the price. I also practiced what I was going to say and how I was going to say it.

The second night, I had seven appointments and sold four. The women paid me cash on the spot. When Peter came to pick me up, I smiled a smile that could've broken my face. We were beside ourselves.

The money we collected went right back into the business. We made the ad bigger.

Peter's phone started ringing, and in no time my appointment book was filled. Twenty women enrolled in the workshop, and it was a success—I knew, because I was being hugged after classes.

After a month, it became apparent that the seminar was becoming very popular. I was renting the studio three nights a week, but the music teacher's business was getting busier, too. We were running into each other and it was becoming a problem (not to mention the fact that we kept rearranging her class and hiding her music stands and books).

Peter and I started looking for another place.

There was space available right across the street. Eight-hundred square feet for $600 a month, but they wanted first and last month's rent. We almost choked. We'd made $1,000 so far through the seminars. It would take that and a bit more to take the space. We did, and moved in.

Now that we had space, we needed a runway. My brother offered his carpentry talents. I put up posters and some blow-ups of my modelling pictures. We bought a few partitions—some made my office, the others made room for accounting, Peter's department. And we moved the phone from Peter's bedroom to the studio.

With the bigger ad, we made enough noise for the media to take notice. Now newspapers and television stations were calling. Consequently, more prospective clients were calling, and the seminars filled up four nights a week.

It was busy. I was busy. I was still modelling, still attending university, and working part-time at a Swiss Chalet restaurant. I needed help. I hired a receptionist, and she sold the workshops and answered the phones while I went out and did the other stuff.

It got even busier in time. By our third year in business, we had to move once again. We took a space down the hall. Now we were up to 2,000 square feet, and we still needed more help. We hired a hairstylist and a make-up artist, both part-time, to help teach the classes. But it wasn't enough.

I knew it was time to reconsider modelling. At any given time I could be sent out to two or three different shoots or runway shows in all parts of the city. I couldn't keep that kind of schedule and run Big, Bold & Beautiful at the same time. I didn't want to let go of our business —we'd be letting too many people down. Then again, I didn't want to let my modelling clients down, either.

We expanded again. But this time, instead of taking on more space, we took on a new venture. We decided to open our own modelling agency, Plus-Figure Models. Clients seemed to think I was the only plus-size model available. We planned to show them differently. We recruited women from our seminars. I taught them how to walk, how to pose and the other necessary ingredients. I wanted to instill in them the kind of confidence I had gained, and show them that they could model at the size they were and the way they were. Then, I stepped back from the spotlight.

Big, Bold & Beautiful was now my number one priority. I quit Swiss Chalet and I slowly let go of my studies (which was hard, but necessary).

Being able to pay much closer attention to the workshops, I realized that plus-size women were constantly complaining about the availability of fashionable clothing. I kept hearing it and hearing it until it started to echo in my head. There was an extraordinary void in the market for attractive, reasonably priced, quality merchandise.

Just about this time, some room became available down the hall. We really didn't have any money for more space—we'd ordered better posters, built a new runway, bought desks and more telephone lines—we had poured everything we made back into the business. Still, I wanted to see this space; I had another idea.

It was small, tiny in fact, but I thought it might serve its purpose. I told Peter I had this idea of starting a small knitwear line. Our clients were telling us that they couldn't find any casual wear, and they were a captive audience. Maybe it was something we should try.

"Do you know how to sew?" Peter asked. I didn't. Neither did he. Where were we going to get this knitwear? I didn't have a clue. (At the time, I had no idea there were manufacturers I could pay to produce it.) So, in our ignorance, we decided to make our own.

"I have a cousin who knows how to sew," Peter offered.

"You do? Bring her in!"

In came Peter's cousin, Felimina. I told her my ideas, she made patterns from scratch, and sewed the clothing in that little studio down the hall. Once again, we used partitions. One quarter of the room was her sewing space, the rest would be the store.

Once the partitions were up, we had to come up with some sort of store layout. Peter suggested we just put up a bar along one wall to hang our merchandise on. That was fine. Then he remembered seeing a cabinet behind the building that someone had left out for garbage. "If you help me drag it up," he said, "we could put it in the corner and use it as a counter." It had glass doors on either side, one of which, he also remembered, had a large crack running up it. "If we sell something," he proposed, "you'll be behind the counter and you'll hide the crack." Fine.

We would also need a cash register. Peter's mother had once owned a jewellery store, and her cash register was still in the basement at home. He warned me it was old—the numbers popped up (it was made well before the invention of receipt tapes or computer chips) and the cash drawer had to be smacked to open. That was fine, too.

So we dragged up the cabinet, brought in the antique cash register, and hung our clothes with their Jackie Jackie labels (which, thanks in part to Felimina, consisted of about fifty different styles). Peter installed some spot-lights and it was done. We stood back, taking in what we had pulled together, feeling very proud.

Time for one more ad: "Big, Bold & Beautiful Boutique, clothing for women with a little extra." Our sizes were 1X, 2X and 3X. Numbering the clothes this way, we thought, was unique and much less intimidating.

Two days after we set up shop, a woman came up the four flights and wandered into the studio where we held our classes. "Hi, I'm looking for Big, Bold & Beautiful Boutique." I overheard her talking to the receptionist and peeked over my partition. "You're looking for what?"

"Big, Bold & Beautiful Boutique," she repeated.

"Are you a customer?"

"Yes," she answered. "Can I see it?"

So far, we had kept the place locked up. I turned to the receptionist. "Carol, do you have the keys?" They were in her desk. "Could you open the door, so I can show this lady the boutique?"

The customer looked around the store, while I took up my position behind the counter and the cracked glass.

Meanwhile, Peter had arrived at the office and was wondering where I was. "She's in the boutique," Carol informed him.

"In the boutique?"

"Yes," she answered, "she has a customer."

"A customer?"

"Yes," she said. "A customer from the *outside.*"

Peter came down and joined me behind the counter. This well-to-do woman was taking her time, scanning the rack. "Can I help you, ma'am?" I asked.

She picked up a long knit dress and said, "Can I try this on?"

I flashed a look at Peter. "Do you need to try it on?" I asked.

"Well," she responded, somewhat surprised, "I'd *like* to try it on."

We'd forgotten about a dressing room. There wasn't one.

"There's a washroom down the hall," Peter offered. "Maybe you'd like to try it on there."

Being the lady she was, she took the dress down the hall to the bathroom without questioning us. When she came back she said, "I love it. I'll take it." We were overjoyed.

"How much is it?" she asked.

I flashed another look at Peter. There were no price tags on anything.

As I had said years ago to my first potential client, once again I spit out, "How much can you afford?"

That woman is still a customer today, which not only pleases me but surprises the hell out of me. Not that our merchandise wasn't worthwhile, but the original presentation was undoubtedly a comedy of errors. When Peter went to pack her dress, it was his turn to flash me a look. There were no bags, there was no tissue. He ran down to the corner store and bought some white Glad kitchen bags while she waited. Then he punched a hole at the top of the bag as a makeshift handle.

It was the start of my education in the hard-knocks school of fashion. We created a change room, we attached price tags, and we got bags to put the clothes in (which, sooner than expected, began flying out of the store).

By this time, Peter's cousin could no longer keep up. She was getting dizzy spells and headaches and was basically stressed out. We needed to hire pattern-makers, graders and cutters—and we did.

This tendency to expand didn't stop. Our efficiently packed boutique was becoming too small. We needed a new home for the entire Big, Beautiful business.

We found another location on Yonge Street. This one was twice the size of our current premises. Not only that, it was on the second floor (that's one flight of stairs versus the four flights we and everyone else were climbing at the time). That, in itself, would be a relief. This place also offered the possibility of splitting the area in two— one half for the workshops, the other half for the boutique. We moved yet again.

Clients, customers and models were climbing up to see us. Clothing manufacturers began venturing up the stairs, too. They were offering to make our Jackie Jackie label for us. This would be another relief, but it wasn't as easy as it sounded.

By this point, our clothing customers were asking why we didn't offer clothes other than our own label. Other manufacturers were offering plus-size clothing—Elizabeth from the American designer Liz Claiborne, Andrea Jovine, among others—but we hadn't thought of asking them in. Now we did.

But, as I said, it wasn't as simple as that. Both the manufacturers who offered to make our line for us and the manufacturers who offered us their own labels had their own ideas. Many of them still held old-fashioned beliefs about plus-size clothing—there had to be bows on everything and it all had to be made of durable, stand-alone, bulletproof polyester. The clothes were awful, and I told them so.

I told them neither their sleeves nor their lengths were long enough for plus-sizes. I would ask well-known plus-size manufacturers why they didn't include the same styles for plus-sizes as they did in their regular lines. That was what I wanted. I wanted the long skirts and the cropped jackets, the short skirts and the same embellishments, buttons and all. I wanted to know why they were keeping those fashion pieces from us.

It got to the point where every time I walked into manufacturers' buying offices, in Canada or the U.S., it felt a little uncomfortable. I knew they were looking at me and thinking, "Oh my God, here she comes, and she's going to demand changes and complain again."

But it didn't stop me. I knew I was the voice of thousands of women, women who didn't have the opportunity to be the middleman. I was talking and shopping for them. I worked on the floor of our boutique and I knew what they wanted and what they were asking for. I would only do business with people who gave me what I wanted—what we all wanted—whether it was my label or someone else's.

While I was harassing manufacturers, we managed to find time to spruce up our new location and build more change rooms (annoyingly necessary things that will probably haunt me for the rest of my life).

As we got bigger, it seemed the media coverage also got bigger.

We were different; they liked that. We were outspoken; that appealed to them too. They were supportive and they were welcomed, but our clients were always our main focus.

We may have talked to the press, but we listened to our shoppers. In fact, we were hyperfocused on them. It was 1989, just about the time Peter and I got married. We took no vacations, except for a one-week honeymoon. Our business was our main concern; in our eyes, we were still getting it off the ground. We still had five years left in that ten-year plan.

Our customers were no longer content with just our knitwear collection. They wanted wool, gabardine and silk. They wanted office wear, outerwear and evening-wear. And they got what they wanted.

With the eveningwear came a new category of customer —mother-of-the-bride. They were so happy to find elegant things in their size but, they said, their poor daughters were having a horrible time looking for larger wedding gowns. I knew what that was like. I had been a glutton for punishment; I had been through the experience twice.

The first time I looked for a wedding dress, it was not the magical moment I had anticipated. Wedding gowns in northern Ontario only went up to size 16, which was a bit tight on me. However, I was young and naive and I thought the one I picked was beautiful for the simple rea-son it was white. I hadn't noticed until I was older that other brides, slimmer brides, had hundreds of gowns to choose from.

The second time I went shopping for a wedding dress, it was downright degrading. At one shop, I was asked to put on a pair of gloves before I could look through the dresses. At another, I was placed in the basement to try on a dress. They brought down a portable mirror for me. When I sneaked back upstairs to grab myself a headpiece, I realized why I was downstairs—a slimmer counterpart was trying on the same dress. I assumed the management didn't want a size 6 to see a size 24 in the same gown. At yet another boutique, I was helped by a saleswoman who yelled to her co-worker, "Doesn't this come any bigger? I need a big one here." And still the choices were few. There was nothing sexy, pretty or dainty about any of them—they simply filled a need.

I had always hoped one day I would open a bridal boutique. I wanted to accommodate other brides with dignity and care, and offer special privileges I thought they needed and deserved. I wanted them to feel like brides, not inconveniences.

I'll never forget the first bride that came into our store. She was forty-five, and it was her first marriage.

She fell in love with an Italian evening suit in ivory silk. It was breathtaking. It was priced at $3,000. The price was extraordinary for us. We really couldn't afford to bring these special pieces in, but we did so in the hope that they would at least spruce up our boutique— and maybe even go to a good home.

The suit fit her like a dream and she decided to take it. Her words were music to my ears. Not only did she look ravishing in it, the suit would make my sales for the week (at least).

Just before I rang in the sale, she said, "It must be wonderful to be married in a wedding dress. I know it may sound silly, I know I'm forty-five, but I would love to be married in a white wedding gown."

I asked her if she had looked for a traditional wedding dress. She told me the largest gown she could find was a size 20. She was a size 24.

The whole time she was talking, I was thinking about the two wedding gowns in the back room—one was a size 26, the other a size 28. I had just bought them. They weren't on the floor. We hadn't set up the bridal area yet.

My heart started to pound. My head was saying, "No!" My heart was screaming, "Yes!" The bridal gowns were priced between $1,200 and $1,300; the suit was more than twice that amount.

"You know what?" I asked. "I have two bridal gowns in the back. They, in fact, may be a little big for you, but they're white and they're beautiful. If you want to try them on, I also have some headpieces." She started to cry.

In the back room, she tried on one of the dresses, I added a crinoline and a headpiece, and she sobbed. She looked beautiful.

"Should I buy it?" she asked.

"If you want to wear it, then you should buy it."

"It's always been my dream," she said. "I want to wear it."

And she did. She bought the wedding dress; I put the ivory suit back on its hanger, and back on display.

The next day, I got a call from her. "I just wanted to tell you how thrilled I am with this wedding gown, how happy I am, and how you made me feel." I was happy she was happy. "But I'm not a stupid woman," she continued. "I know you didn't have to tell me about the wedding gowns in the back. I know the suit I was going to buy cost $2,000 more. I still need a going-away outfit. I'm coming in today to buy the suit."

I knew it was important to be able to truly empathize with a customer. I knew how important it was to have a variety of styles; to have a variety of sizes so a bride could experience the feeling of that zipper going up the back; to have privacy. I knew it was important for a bride to feel beautiful the way she was, not when she lost the thirty pounds she planned to take off before the wedding—that's how other bridal retailers felt. It was important to let them know they were wonderful just the way they were—the way their fiances fell in love with them—and if they lost or gained weight it didn't matter; alterations could be made. Quite simply, it's a sensitive and stressful time that needs kid-glove treatment.

With all that in mind, we made room for a bridal boutique.

At the same time, the modelling agency was growing. Advertisers didn't want one model anymore, they wanted three or four at the same time. My roster grew to thirty models.

Big, Bold & Beautiful was not just growing, it was swelling. It was 1991 and we were back out on the pavement looking for another home.

We found home sweet home. We spied the perfect spot in Toronto's exclusive Yorkville area—a two-level building with room for all of us on street level. This was it. Plus-Figure Models could take the top floor; Big, Bold & Beautiful Boutique would occupy the main floor. There was only one hitch; we still had a year left on our current lease, and we'd have to pay to get out of it. It was a tough decision, but we did it. We did it for our customers who had been climbing the stairs for years, we did it for our staff, and we did it for the media—people who never once balked at how or where we ran the business.

Running the business, however, changed a little at the new location. Because the modelling agency was growing to gargantuan proportions, it was taking time and space away from our seminars. We decided to scale down the workshops by only offering personal-development programs on occasion.

Still, having an expansive new location didn't stop everything else from expanding. In the boutique, we had casual wear, office wear, eveningwear, outerwear and bridal wear. Only one thing was missing—innerwear. To begin with, we needed bustiers to go under bridal gowns. And when intimate apparel manufacturers came to visit, I couldn't help but notice all the other frilly items. So I started to carry camisoles, teddies, negligées, bras and panties and peignoirs.

The customers went nuts. They wanted more. They wanted things I never imagined. They wanted the risqué —thongs, garter belts, fishnet stockings and merry widows. I wondered what I had turned them into. It got to a point where I couldn't keep crotchless panties in stock. These women were wild, hot and willing to go the distance.

But then, there had been a time when there were no luxurious, self-indulgent choices. There was a time, years past, when there was nothing but utilitarian garments. It didn't surprise me that these women—my customers—wanted the exotic in everything imaginable.

However, not everyone does. Very recently, a woman I had never seen before came into the shop. After looking through the undergarments, she turned and said, "You don't have anything in polyester." I shook my head. "I really wanted something in nylon or polyester," she explained, "but all of your things are cotton, silk or charmeuse."

She told me the plus-size chain she normally shopped at had gone out of business, and she had travelled five hours from Ottawa just to buy a polyester nightgown. I was sorry to disappoint her, but told her I would look into it.

I did and I bought a few. Since then, which wasn't long ago, I've had similar requests for caftan-like nighties from other women—women who also had been left stranded by the demise of that plus-size clothing chain. Even though I personally wouldn't wear something like that, obviously I now have customers who do.

Big, Bold & Beautiful began on the premise that plus-size women can and should have everything they could possibly want. I can fill my store with beautiful things. I can try to educate the customer into believing she is sexy and worthwhile enough to swathe herself in luscious fabrics and sophisticated style—but I can't do anymore than that.

Sizing-up fashion

Imagine, if you will, that you are watching television. During a commercial break, a close-up of an attractive woman comes into view. Seductively, she looks into the camera.

"Some men will try to tell you that more than a handful is wasteful," she muses.

"But then," she continues with a knowing smile, "you know what they say about men with small hands."

The camera pans back, exposing the fact that this woman is indeed sexy, voluptuous and plus-size. The commercial ends with the slogan: Size is never an issue at Big, Bold & Beautiful Boutique.

It's not a run-of-the-mill television ad. Cheekiness aside, the very fact that the commercial deals with plus-sizes is unusual in itself. I thought it was pretty unusual the first time I saw it. But then, seeing myself on television is never an entirely comfortable thing. However, portraying that cheeky woman, who seductively looks into the camera, was comfortable. The woman in the commercial is me, and God knows she is a far cry from the same woman I was many years ago (the other one wouldn't have dared talk about her size or sexiness, let alone broadcast it).

Because you never see anything like this on television, because largeness and sexiness are never shown together, and because plus-size women have been stereotyped so negatively for so long, we wanted to attack these issues with an in-your-face, all-out wink and nudge.

We live in a very visual society; regardless of how unfortunate that may seem, it's true. However, we wanted to use that to our advantage.

With continuous play of plus-size commercials as powerful as this one, we thought we could prove to larger women who felt somewhat neglected by the fashion industry that they were in fact noticed and esteemed through positive image reinforcement via television.

Obviously, not everyone is thin, tall, blonde, younger than twenty-five and a size 8. Hit the malls, hit the streets, visit your favourite restaurant—it's hard to ignore the fact that we all come in different sizes, shapes, colours and ages. The larger category, however, is made to feel a little guiltier about being different than the rest.

In a big city where hosts of fitness, health and beauty experts make fortunes helping people work toward some physical ideal, a large size woman can feel totally out of the fashion loop. In a city where a thin woman frets over the ill effects of a piece of birthday cake, what chance does a size 24 have to find self-acceptance, let alone a fashion identity?

For ages, the plus-size woman was catered to by an ignorant fashion industry that provided only shoddy, horrible merchandise—a direct insult to her intelligence.

Plenty has changed over the past several years. A new wave of plus-size retailers, armed with fresh points of view and the instincts of true merchants, is making fashion a positive experience for larger women.

Ask anyone in the fashion business today what the plus-size customer wants, needs and thinks and you will get a number of fast answers. Those in the fashion world know a lot more than they used to. When we first got into the business, however, plus-size manufacturers were sure of only one thing—their customers wouldn't wear bright colours, large prints, stirrup pants, bustiers or anything sexy. But our customers started wearing these items and demanding more, and we knew better than to believe those old myths.

One of the changes I can't help but notice, dealing with thousands of women every year, is being plus-size has become a state of mind rather than a temporary state.

For decades, many women believed being big was simply a passing phase. They didn't want to make a long-term investment in clothing, because as far as they were concerned their situation wasn't going to be long-term. They would shop at certain large-chain stores and buy cheaper clothing to fill a momentary need. They'd pick up a suit for $100. The women were happy, and so were the stores' salespeople. The retailers knew from statistics she'd be back: first of all, their merchandise would only last about a year; secondly, the chances were slim that she would be slim by the time the suit started to fall apart. These clothing stores were reaping the benefits; the plus-size woman was not.

In all fairness to those narrow-minded retailers (who stereotyped big women as lazy, sloppy, dirty and down-right ugly), attitudes and opinions change rather rapidly in North America. When it comes to fashion, they change at the speed of light. Unfortunately, these retailers were a tad slow in coming up to speed.

The myth that plus-sizes don't care about fashion is just that. Taste does not shrink in direct proportion to an increase in dress size. Large women know the difference between fashionable and frumpy.

Something that became very obvious in the early days at our boutique was our customers were not looking for stop-gap clothing. The most fashion-forward items did not end up on sale racks. They sold—no matter what the price. Sure, to most shoppers price is a prime concern, but we found our clients didn't base their choices on price; they targetted clothing that signalled dignity and respect. They wanted to look together right then and there. They weren't waiting for the ultimate size 8 woman to emerge.

There's no denying people are treated with more dignity and respect when they look good. They demand a different kind of attention and better treatment. Better treatment feeds self-esteem and forces us to demand more in our interactions with others. It also helps us realize we deserve the best life has to offer.

Looking great—dressing in clothes we like and feel sexy and confident in—is another stepping stone. It's the first step in proving to ourselves and the rest of the world that we've come out from hiding. We're out of the closet. Frankly, considering the amount of time we've spent in the closet, it's a wonder we're not all impeccable dressers—we've certainly had plenty of time to mix, match and test ideas.

And, experimenting with personal style is key. It can be extremely beneficial to alter the image you put forward to the world—cool and professional during the day, romantic or sultry at night.

However, achieving personal style is not always easy in a sometimes claustrophobic fashion climate. One of the worst excesses of the fashion world is its tendency to pigeon-hole and generalize. They tell us big women shouldn't wear short skirts, short women shouldn't wear long skirts, and so on, and so on. What bunk!

This stuff infuriates me. If we followed the gospel laid down by so-called fashion gurus, we'd be left with nothing to wear but our birthday suits. Opinions like these only inhibit women from flaunting their best features (whether it be their gams or their cleavage) and letting their imaginations run rampant.

Fantasy is part of the fashion world. (This, of course, is painfully obvious in fashion magazines, but where it's really meant to be is in your wardrobe, not on their glossy pages.) Size doesn't have to be an issue when clothes are entrance-making. Let's face it, being plus-size is an attention-getter in itself. Why not embellish that by wearing something that adds ambience and drama? I've always found by doing this people don't really notice size—they just stand up and take notice.

Granted, it's easy for me to say that now. But I can't deny the fact that I once lived by the rules of drab, shabby style.

Back then, I thought of myself as a rather poor investment. Why buy clothes when eventually I would be thinner and need a whole new wardrobe anyway? I was
planning to get thin for the summer, for Christmas, for
Easter, forever, for everyone, except me. "Tomorrow"
was my theme song. But tomorrow never came, and I
never bought myself anything nice.

Whenever I did shop for the necessities, I thought
poor fit was my fault. My body was out of proportion;
the construction of the garment was never in question.
Consequently, most of my shopping trips ended in tears
and self-disgust.

Besides that, I had tunnel vision—I didn't want to
experiment with clothes, and I didn't want anyone helping me. I had a fixed way of dressing and I stuck to it.
No doubt, modelling forced me to widen my scope. I
had a whole slew of people dressing me in different
ways, seeing me in different lights. It was forced exper-
imentation, I'll admit, but it helped me look at myself
from another angle, and it helped me shop for clothes.

Even though developing your own style can be trying,
and at times discouraging, it needn't be. I thought of it
as another challenge, a new adventure.

Working on your outward image first brings an immediate boost. However, as with everything, developing
your style is not an overnight miracle, it's actually an evo-
lutionary process that goes on forever. It requires time.

Basically, it's a lifelong expedition of exploring new
and exciting ways to decorate and adorn your fullness
and view your entire being with pleasure in a full-length
mirror.

When I decided to look at clothing from another
angle, one of the first things I did was treat myself with

respect by spending my hard-earned dollars on quality merchandise. I didn't use the cover of *Vogue* as my yardstick of quality, as much as I focused on having the right clothes for the right moments.

And, over the years, I came up with a few guidelines that helped me come to terms with my size and my new found body acceptance while I was shopping.

I promised myself I would never wear ill-made or ill-fitting clothes. I also noted that trying to feel smaller in smaller sizes never worked. Besides, a size is only a number. I knew a woman was truly confident when she accepted and was comfortable with her actual body size.

I also kept a close eye on my closet. I tried to remain reasonably up-to-the-minute and fashionable. Hanging onto old clothes, I figured, was not helpful. Not only did they look dated, but by the time they came back into fashion again I'd usually had time to reconsider their style (bell-bottoms are a prime example).

I also refused to wear anything old, dirty or in need of repair. I was only too aware that such items fed into society's warped and ugly stereotypes of large women.

When it came to actually being in a clothing store, I decided to give unfamiliar styles a bit of time in the mirror. I'd play around with them. Would it look better with different accessories, with different shoes, maybe with a different belt?

One of the most freeing guidelines I set for myself was to never, ever rely on criticism or any horrible fat-phobic rules to influence my wardrobe selection. I'm glad I did. There would be a lot of stuff hanging in my closet today that I wouldn't be able to wear if I had let fashion critics rule me. And, thank you, but I'm old enough to dress myself.

We got big, we didn't get dumb. When we see something on the rack that has hanging threads or an uneven hemline, we don't buy it. However, when we spot a well-designed garment, it makes our heart skip a beat and our lips smile with pride.

I learned from past experience there was nothing daunting about looking in a mirror. I knew it wasn't going to make me look fatter or slimmer. I wasn't afraid of seeing a large woman in the reflection, but I *was* concerned about seeing a large, unkempt woman in the mirror (just as I would have been afraid to see a thin, dowdy woman standing there). I let my heart lead the way. If I wanted to wear bright printed outfits, leggings or a string bikini, I was no longer waiting for someone's approval. I wore what I wanted.

When we shop for clothes, it's essential to believe that we deserve beautiful things. As far as I'm concerned, this is the best tip I ever gave myself.

Unfortunately, quite a few plus-size women shop with the attitude that they will be disappointed, because they've been let down before. They think nothing will fit and nothing will look good. But I found it was better to completely dismiss any negative thoughts. "I can hardly wait to try this on, it's going to look fabulous," was much more effective than, "If I put it on it's going to be too tight or too short, and it will look just awful." In the beginning shopping was intimidating, but I knew I had to give myself permission to look my best. At the very least, I needed to give myself the option of trying something on to see if it looked good.

Of course, good clothing is not cheap. But the reverse is also true: cheap clothing is not good. We all know this. We've been there. We used to visit store after store, looking for anything on a hanger that was reasonably acceptable. Anything that fit. If you were lucky enough to locate a pair of pull-on, polyester pants that didn't look too terrible, you bought them in three or four different colours. You bought in bulk. It wasn't a pleasure, and it certainly wasn't fashion. Manufacturers and retailers held to the belief that as soon as a woman passed a size 16, she was short on taste and happy to skip merrily into bulletproof, stand-alone polyester heaven.

Times fortunately are changing. It's now possible to find beautifully made clothes with style and pizazz. Manufacturers have evolved. But large-size fashion will only go as far as we're willing to take it. If we demand quality and choices, we'll get them.

Today, I find it all quite amusing. Designers are actually competing against one another with sumptuous fabrics, impeccable workmanship and avant-garde styles—the height of fashion. The only reason they're getting better is because they're getting smarter, and for the first time in a long time they are, in fact, in competition. They've finally realized plus-size women have a lot of money to spend—in North America alone there are more than 36 million of us—and we're willing to spend, but we're getting fussy. We've sent them all into a tizzy. Before, if they so much as offered anything more exciting than a pair of polyester pants, we'd eat it up. They threw us treats, and we obediently jumped for them. But we're not jumping anymore. We know we deserve to be treated all the time (like anyone else). And now they know if they want our money, they're the ones who have to jump.

NINE

A Model Image

SMALL TOWNS HOLD a different concept of beauty. It's quite unique. In fact, small-town attitudes of beauty are not entirely dissimilar from feminist opinions; however, we never looked at it in those terms (we weren't acquainted with feminist values—or feminists for that matter).

In the country, I looked at myself as being a very wholesome girl. I didn't find a need for make-up. There wasn't a reason to cover up. As a teenager I would occasionally wear lipstick, but very little. I hardly ever did anything to my hair. I had a fresh country look. I didn't think of ways to enhance it, I just enjoyed the natural beauty I had.

Of course, I was also affected by my peers; they didn't wear make-up, either. And, growing up in a European family (a mix of Canadian, Polish and French backgrounds), I didn't even think I could experiment with the stuff. It was a no-no. Only bad girls wore make-up.

I really didn't know anything about cosmetics. I certainly didn't see that much on people around me, and I didn't watch enough television to think that our country ways were unusual. I just enjoyed being the person I was, packaging included.

But, of course, it was a different story in the city. The big city was filled with another approach to beauty altogether. Make-up, hairdos, lip gloss, hairspray, bobbles, bangles, beads—it was startling. To be acceptable, you had to dress in a certain way, wear make-up just so, and do your hair like everyone else.

This big-city concept was obvious. I could see it in the malls, even riding on the bus. There was barely a soul who didn't have her face entirely decked out. It was culture shock to me.

At the time, however, I wasn't feeling terrific about myself. Still, in my heart I knew I was beautiful, but I just couldn't be bothered to play their game. In fact, I couldn't be bothered with my natural beauty either. I had my caftans and my tent dresses, my scarves and my kerchiefs. I was not showing myself to my fullest potential whatsoever; I was in hiding. If I could have found a way, I'm sure I would have hid my face, too. And I don't mean hiding in the figurative sense. I was literally hiding—I was more or less a recluse for a year.

Being stuck in the house, I couldn't help but watch television and leaf through a few magazines. There, on the screen and on the pages, I saw this other concept of beauty. After a while, I started to see it in the same way you view a Christmas tree. People didn't just buy an evergreen and throw it in the corner; they decorated it, they enhanced it and, in a way, it made sense to enhance natural beauty. I was coming to terms with this new found sense of beauty, but I still wasn't trying it on.

When I started attending university, my peers were teenagers. Not only was I somewhat older than them, I was a tad larger, and I felt like a bit of an outcast. The kids weren't heavily into make-up, but they did dress differently than I did. So I cleaned up my act. I got rid of the scarves, I washed my hair more frequently and I used a touch of lipstick.

I realized to be truly accepted in this academic environment—or in the city at large—I had to do something about myself. I didn't have a lot of money, particularly after I separated from my husband, but I did what I could. It wasn't a natural progression for me; it was more of a forced progression, but I knew to be admitted into this society, I had to do what everyone else was doing. Slowly but surely, I started to take a bit better care of myself. Not a heck of a lot, but a little better care.

Previously, I had thought that by not taking care, by concealing myself in kerchiefs and caftans, I would blend into the crowd. I would go unnoticed. However, I learned very quickly that this was having the reverse effect—not taking care was actually making me stand out all the more.

I thought if I added a bit of make-up and fixed my hair, I might be left alone. So I started working with make-up and my hair. I wasn't *playing* with make-up and my hair—that would imply I was getting a sense of pleasure from it. I did it because it was suddenly necessary.

Oddly enough, it had an effect. I was being treated differently—better. Because of these results, taking care of myself was not such a big issue. It felt less and less like a required exercise, and I began to experiment more.

When I was asked to take part in the fashion show for that plus-size boutique, it became another turning point. There were about twenty of us participating as models. The owner had hired make-up artists and hairstylists to groom us, and when they were finished we looked like a room full of movie stars. I felt so wonderful. I realized at the size I was I could be truly beautiful.

At the same time, I met Peter. I was twenty-five, a size 24, and still not entirely sure of myself. I wasn't wearing a lot of make-up, and I wasn't fixing my hair in any elaborate style. Nonetheless, Peter felt I was beautiful the way I was. He managed to see through my inability to put on make-up or do my hair expertly. He looked through all that and saw me.

He also thought I was pretty wonderful on the runway, and asked if I had ever considered being a professional model. Not only was it the furthest thing from my mind, I'd never heard of a large woman being a model.

He told me there were plus-size models in the U.S., and showed me some photos. That was all well and good, I mentioned, but he was overlooking the fact that there were still no plus-size models in Canada. I reminded him of how conservative Canadians are. "I'm large," I said. "They'll laugh." He suggested we try it anyway.

Because we didn't have any money for a professional photographer, Peter took me to the beach at Toronto's lakefront and took pictures himself. He posed me, he shot the photos, and he developed the film. Then he introduced me to his agent. We explained we hadn't had the money for professional photos, and hoped Peter's would suffice.

"As you know, plus-size modelling isn't predominant here," she responded. "We've had a few girls do a few shows, but we really haven't promoted the category." Nonetheless, she decided to give it a shot. She'd send my photos to some of her clients and see how it went.

The agency called me by my last name, Hope. They thought it would be inspirational. The name and the idea caught on. I started to get bookings—the department stores (Eaton's, The Bay, Sears) wanted me for catalogues—and it happened fast.

It was marvellous, but it was also mystifying. Not long before this moment, I had been a despondent housewife who hid in sacks and scarves. In a few short days, I would be standing in front of a camera portraying big was beautiful.

It was a curious, conflicted turn of fate. I had been married to a man who told me I had something wrong with me; I was larger, therefore unattractive. Now I had a man on my arm telling me how beautiful I was. And, very soon, I would be standing in front of a camera for millions of people to see.

The whole issue left me in complete turmoil, and I lay in bed for days. I kept thinking I would rather have been able to stand in front of the camera the way I used to be: a fresh and natural country girl with no worries about make-up or hairdos or body size, untouched and unblemished by society. But I would have to wear make-up and do my hair and stand there. It was required by this society. And my form of approval would be the clicking of the camera. I thought, in city culture, this route was the only way to acceptance.

Not surprisingly, this time in my life now seems like a bit of a blur. Nonetheless, I do have some very vivid memories. One of my first jobs was to take part in a fashion show at a downtown Toronto mall, The Eaton

Centre. I remember the stylist for the show was ecstatic about using a plus-size model. It was a first for her; it was a first for me, too.

I'll never forget how I shook, waiting to go on. I wasn't in the first scene, which comprised string bikinis and fur coats, but I was in the second, which featured business suits. I stood next to a regular-size model; we would walk out together. My heart was pounding, and I was wondering how people would react. I looked like the woman standing next to me; I just had an extra seventy pounds. I kept trying to convince myself everything would be all right.

Then our cue came. Although that runway was only fifteen feet long, it seemed about one hundred. There was a group of children on the floor at the end of the runway looking up at me. I tried not to stare ahead—like a deer caught in headlights—I tried to glance around. Everyone was smiling, but they also seemed to be scratching their heads, as if to say, "How did this woman get on the runway? Is she loose?" Obviously, I wasn't something they were used to.

This wasn't something I was used to either. As I was walking, I was thinking, "God, I just want to run." I tried to remind myself I was doing this to prove something. I was making a physical statement. But the whole time, this voice in my head was screaming, "What are you doing?! I don't want to be here! Get off the stage!"

It's astonishing to me that I found the courage to make it down the runway and back up again; it's astonishing that I continued modelling.

My first photo session was equally nerve-racking. I was to pose for the Canadian department store, Simpsons. I hadn't posed for a camera in years, except for my

brief experience with Peter. I knew Peter, I was comfortable with him. Now I would be posing for and with
strangers. This was completely different. I would stand
in front of a photographer and a stylist, and beside a
thinner model.

In the change room, getting ready for the shoot, I
mimicked everything I saw my thinner counterpart do,
because I hadn't the foggiest idea about modelling pro-
tocol. I saw her powdering her face, so I pulled out my
powder. I was in my underwear, because she was in her
underwear, and I understood this was what you did to
avoid getting make-up on the clothes. As all this was
going on, the stylist came in.

She said hello to both of us and then turned to me.
"I think it's terrific that we're starting to include plus-
size models, but you know, Hope, you really should
lose weight. You're really fat." Well, this threw me for a
loop. It must have showed on my face because she continued, "I think size 18 is too big. You should get down
to a 16. Eighteen is too much. We don't want to surprise
people. We just want to sneak it in. That way, you won't
frighten them."

I was standing in my underwear, and the stylist had
just told me I was fat. It certainly was no surprise to me
that I was overweight, but how was I supposed to go in
front of the camera with a smile on my face, knowing
that the very person who hired me thought I was too big
for the picture.

I had no idea if she was being cruel or if she was
merely one of those people who had an uncanny knack
of making me feel inferior (like my first husband). Nonetheless, regardless of her motives, if she had any, I was
now in the position of having to fight for the energy to

put on those clothes and smile sweetly. The whole time, that little voice screamed, "I'm huge. I'm a barge. What am I doing here? I hate modelling!"

I knew I was pretty enough for the camera—I was wearing all the required make-up and hairspray—but, obviously, there was just too much prettiness happening, an expanse of prettiness, shall we say. I had a tremendous fear they were going to call my agent and tell her they had to reshoot with a smaller model (which was ridiculous, because there weren't any smaller plus-size models; I was it). I left that day with my tail between my legs, panicked about what to do.

I watched what I ate and slimmed down to a size 16. No one else commented again. Not until a few months later.

I was hired to model in a fashion show. This time I was told, "I think you should gain some weight. If you want to be accepted by the audience, they have to see that you're significantly larger."

Yet again, my life was becoming one large amusement park. Up and down, round and round, and loop the loop —step right up, buy your ticket and take your chances.

I was secure; I was insecure. And back and forth. The only thing I didn't worry about was my hair and make-up. I had that down pat. But my body image was completely distorted. And for years, I went up and down the rack of sizes.

Only when I stopped modelling did I truly start to enjoy my face and body, because the pressure was off. I didn't have to run into a change room before an appointment and check the tag to see what size the outfit was. I did this because I was petrified that the garment wouldn't fit. Stylists insisted on laying out size 10s, when they knew full well I was a size 16. I'd have to squeeze into these things. I was on constant lookout for labels—was it going to do up, was the skirt going to fit, would the blouse button? My nerves were forever on edge. No one seemed to know anything about plus sizes. They just couldn't relate to anything over a size 8.

In those early years, it was hard not to notice some stylists just didn't want to relate. I'd overhear them snickering, "Oh my God! Those pants are huge!" There were times I walked down runways and heard snorting or oinking. I didn't hear it all the time, but I heard it. What was more important, however, was what I didn't hear. I might have gotten, "Here she is, accept her," but I never got, "Isn't she pretty? Look at her hair. Look at her face." I wasn't a woman; I was a product.

I accepted this, to a degree. I knew I was representing a large proportion of society, and whatever I did was helping somehow. That, in itself, made it okay. It wasn't hypocritical. I wasn't doing it because I had money in my pocket when I was through. I wasn't doing it to get through university. I was doing it because, in my heart of hearts, I knew someone out there would feel good because they saw me. If anyone said, "Hey, she's doing it. I can do it, too," it would have been worth it.

So I curled my fists, bit my lip and kept moving. I knew there would be a happy ending, I just had to swim against the current. I had to prove to the clients, agents, stylists, choreographers, readers or viewers, and gawkers that I deserved to be there. There were a lot of people like me out there—maybe their sister, their mother, their brother, their cousin or their aunt—and they deserved not only to be seen but to be represented. If I kept fighting—and I would keep fighting—eventually I'd win.

At home, away from the spotlights, I thought of myself as an attractive woman. My knees certainly didn't tremble at my beauty, and I was in no way vain about my looks, but I was happy with them. I was happy when people lined up to ask me questions and tell me they liked what I did. The contentment came from my actions, not from my looks. It may sound manipulative, but I simply used my looks to get what I wanted. I never looked in the mirror and said, "Thumbs up! You look hot!" I considered it a business arrangement. I used my looks to get results, just as anyone would use a talent to get a job done.

However, I never looked in the mirror and said, "Yuck." I merely looked in the mirror to experiment further with myself—to be more current or to alter the image in different ways.

Besides, I was still dealing with the occasional snort and oink. I felt I was preparing myself to be a stronger person. I was doing whatever it took—perfecting the make-up, arranging the hair, adjusting the body—to keep going. But what I didn't realize was this route was, in fact, never ending. It wasn't like university, where you could complete your studies, get a diploma and say, "Yes! I'm finished!" I was never finished.

However, it was like that old saying, "When in Rome...." I lived where I lived, and I did what was expected to make my visions a reality. My dream was not the cover of *Vogue*; I was hoping to be an advocate. I wasn't fighting for me alone. And, I wasn't just fighting so one day someone like me could be on the cover of *Vogue*. I suppose I was fighting because I couldn't see anyone else doing it at the time. No one else wanted to do it. They knew it was a big battle, and they were tired.

But if this was what it took for me to make a point, then that's what it took. Underneath the warpaint and the light bulbs was a simple hope for acceptance. Not an acceptance of hair and make-up or being fashionable; acceptance of size.

Through all this, I realized the clients were frightened to venture further. They had gambled on one plus-size model and that was enough for them. I was expected to fill all of their ads and all of their needs—from sizes 16 to 24. They may have thought that was just fine, but it wasn't just fine with me. They could have control over the make-up and the hair, but I'd be damned if they were going to continue their reign over my body. I had no idea why I had let them dictate the rules and the sizes. They wanted me at a size 12, 18 *and* 24. What they wanted was more models. I knew there had to be an agency with women of different sizes and shapes, so I could get off this ferris wheel. So I decided to start one.

I told my agent. She praised the idea and said it was the right time, the perfect time. I knew it was about time.

There was a stereotypical image in the modelling industry that plus-size women didn't know how to take care of themselves, didn't know anything about hair and make up, and were slovenly. Other agencies definitely had no interest in grooming these women.

We knew differently. We had a list of examples. Women who had come to our seminars and discovered their natural attributes and how to enhance them. That's what our business was based on.

In the seminars, we believed it was important to let plus-size women know they were extremely beautiful at the size they were and the way they were. The know-how and how-tos of make-up and hair only heightened that. But the building blocks of beauty were far more important—the almond eyes, the high cheekbones, the full mouth, whatever it was that made a woman unique.

It was a key point for me as an instructor and a model. Underneath it all, I really did think I was pretty. The country-girl feeling I had may have been hidden, but it was always there. It was this foundation that let me portray what the clients expected.

When I opened the agency, I looked for prospective models in malls, in restaurants and in the street, as well as at the seminars.

One woman came in to see about our program. She was about twenty-two years old, and something about her made me stop and notice. She hung her head a little lower than usual. She had a stain on her blouse and a pin held one of her button-holes together. She had roots showing in her hair and buck teeth. Still, there was something about her that interested me. I brought her into my office and asked if she had ever considered modelling. "Me? No. I couldn't do that," she said. "I just want to learn how to clean myself up and look better."

I couldn't help but be fond of her. I taught her different ways of doing her hair and make-up, how to dress appropriately and how to take care of her clothes, even if it was just one outfit. Today, she's a very confident woman. In fact, she's with the Elite modelling agency in Chicago and with the Wilhemina agency in New York; she's one of my top models.

It's very rewarding to help a woman gain self-confidence and assuredness, and watch her go on to other things, whatever the endeavour.

And it was rewarding to realize that, in some way, I had become that advocate I had wanted to be. I honestly believed in all our models. I was told by other agents that I babied them, held their hands too much, looked out and spoke up for them too often. I was supposed to be hard on them. It was gibberish. I knew what it was like at the other end of the camera, and I knew the insecurities that arose. I wasn't going to tell a model she wasn't beautiful the way she was, and I wasn't going to say she needed to change.

Yes, it's true, to be accepted in our society it's important to look a certain way. Outside packaging counts. It may seem ridiculous, but in our culture it's what's expected and accepted.

On a certain level it's still very silly to me, but just because I find it silly at times, I can't change it, nor can I ignore it.

I have come to see it all as I once viewed my collection of dolls. Fashion and beauty have become fun. I can wake up each morning and, depending on my mood, I can look a certain way. It simply enhances my multifaceted personality.

If I feel like wearing a sweatshirt and sweatpants, I still have to be presentable. I won't wear make-up, but I'll wash my hair, and if I have a pimple on my face, I'll cover it. That simple.

It's just about being presentable. And, it's become just another expectation I have of myself — not an expectation of society — just like taking a shower or brushing my teeth. I don't want another year to slide by without bringing out the best part of me. There were years that slid by when I didn't give myself the opportunity to put my best foot forward. I deserve to look good; this is not something reserved only for my thinner counterparts.

It's vitally important to take care of yourself now, and to give yourself license to look beautiful—to experiment with hair and make-up and not wait for that size 8. However, if you truly don't want to wear your hair in a current style, wear the latest trends, or put on make-up, c'est la vie. Don't do it. The most important thing is to be happy with who you are.

I just have this feeling that the majority of plus-size women put their lives on hold, feeling they can't be attractive or don't deserve to be attractive until they lose weight. This is a major mistake. You can't possibly start liking yourself if you don't take care of yourself. And you can't possibly expect respect from the world around you if you don't feel you're the best you can be.

Size has nothing to do with fashion or beauty. It's possible to not want to play the fashion game, but it's also possible to be up-to-the-minute fashionable if that's your desire. Fashion magazines are not for slim people alone. Even though they don't appear to have a realistic image figured into their game plan, it doesn't mean the reader hasn't figured out her own image and realized: the clothing is available in larger sizes; the make-up can be applied to any face; the hairstyles can be adapted to any head; and, the attitude can be carried off by anyone.

We have to remember to indulge ourselves—to treat ourselves to clothing and make-up—just because, not only when we've earned it. When you start treating yourself with dignity and respect, you start feeling a lot better about yourself. Life is not something to be put on hold. Beauty does not stop at a size 14.

Without a doubt, beauty is about feeling good. It became obvious, as I started feeling more confident, I was going to the dentist more often and visiting the doctor on a regular basis, not only because I cared about my appearance, but because I cared about my well-being. I wanted to ensure if I looked attractive on the outside, I was also healthy on the inside.

Beauty also means good health. This is something that some pass off, not realizing that the latest hair treatment or hottest shade of lipstick won't do the trick if the patient is not in fine order. It's about plenty of sleep, healthy eating and exercise. Beauty includes a clear complexion, shiny hair and strong teeth, but these things don't come out of a bottle. If you don't take care of the basics, you can forget about the lotions, potions and concealers—they won't compensate for an unhealthy lifestyle.

And a healthy lifestyle includes coddling. Pampering is at the very root of looking good and feeling fine. I know, I've pampered myself an awful lot.

I used to listen to soft music while scented candles burned around the room. I used this time to fantasize. I wouldn't dream about a small shape or a thin body, but think of myself in different situations, ones I wasn't yet able to handle in the real world—speaking in front of a large audience with no inhibitions about my size or myself, and other visions where size was not an issue.

I would give myself a facial, manicure or pedicure. I always loved knowing I had ten toes painted red and pampered. No one else saw them, it was just for me.

I would also relax in the hot tub at the health club. One of the nice things about this treat was watching the many shapes and sizes coming in for a soak. The focus of these women was to soothe themselves, without thinking their tummies were too big, their breasts sagged or their bottoms had too many dimples. It was refreshing to see there were all types and forms of women who felt good about their bodies and exposed it.

All these things had the added benefit of fostering an inner beauty. I wanted to find that beauty, underneath the make-up and the hairspray. The outside beauty was available at any cosmetic counter; finding inner beauty meant digging a little deeper. I knew once the make-up came off and the hairspray came out, I'd be left in front of the mirror. And I had to see someone there who was worth it.

Everything I did was a form of therapy. I took a long, hot bath. Of course anyone can take a long, hot bath, but I wasn't satisfied with just that. I'd get out of the tub and slather luxurious body lotion all over. Then, I'd slip under the covers to watch my favourite soap opera. And, for once, I wouldn't feel guilty. I never wondered what I was doing loafing in bed, naked, swathed in lotion, incredibly comfortable. I knew what I was doing—I was getting in touch with myself.

I also got in touch with myself literally. It may sound silly, but I would go to a flower shop, buy myself a bouquet and have it sent to me. There had been so many years when I barely heard a kind word, however I knew it was important to know others felt dearly about you. So, I'd send a card along: "To a special person, who is beautiful inside and out."

I would do that occasionally, because it would make me feel good to come home to flowers on my doorstep. Obviously, they were from me, but in a way they felt like they were coming from someone else. They were from that hidden person inside who knew I was beautiful. It was like reaching out and taking hold of my own hand and saying, "It's okay. You are beautiful. This is a little treat for you. Enjoy."

Anything I did proved I was worth it.

There are too many insecurities that raise their ugly, little heads every day in our lives, and when you have variables around you that make you think you're less than you are, you have to prove otherwise. You can't wait for someone else to prove it; you have to prove it to yourself.

I was so tired of wanting and waiting. These were very strong words in my vocabulary. I *wanted* to be liked; I *waited* to be liked.

I started celebrating my beauty and brought whatever was inside me out, so I, and everyone else, could look at myself and say, "She really is confident. She's a beautiful woman." And I would be that beautiful woman from within; size wasn't the issue.

At the bottom of it all, it's what's inside that counts. If you are not confident and self-assured, beautifying will be merely a vain pursuit of false and empty wishes—a mere carcass or painting of a beautiful woman with the soul, mind and heart of a thin woman trying to get out. I didn't have a thin woman in me trying to get out. I had a beautiful woman trying to get out.

There's no denying, beauty starts from within and radiates throughout. If you feel good about yourself, you will present the most beautiful person you are to the world. You will feel like taking care of yourself and pampering yourself physically and mentally, because you'll believe you are worthwhile.

My original view of attractiveness may have readjusted over the years, but my early beliefs about beauty have never left me. Beauty is made up of many things: voice, movement, grooming, body language, personality, attitude, posture, mannerisms, lifestyle, ambitions and identity.

It may seem like a long-winded definition, but it's really quite simple. A beautiful woman is someone who oozes self-confidence, has her own personal style, believes in herself, walks with poise, and shows the world that beauty can't be measured. There are no limits.

TEN

Big Shots

THERE WAS A TIME when mentors were awesome and thoughtful people— Martin Luther King, Gandhi and Mother Teresa are only a few that come to mind. However, people's greatness is not always measured by their thoughtfulness anymore, and those worthy of looking up to are harder to come by. To compensate, I offer a few fine words from fellow human beings. Good words from good people—possible candidates for new and realistic role models.

Do not put your life on hold, waiting to be a size you are not genetically programmed to be. Do not accept size discrimination. Fight back whenever you can, in whatever means you are comfortable with. You will feel so much better, and you will make it easier for those who come behind you.

—Frances M. White, President, National Association to Advance Fat Acceptance (NAAFA)

The main concern is to know who you are. If you want to change who you are, fine. If you don't, that's fine too. But know who you are, and be who you are. It's important to do that, and not get caught up in the images of the world.

I stopped grappling with this issue when I decided I wanted to lose weight–not because I was trying to look like anyone else. I decided I wanted to do something with my body. I started walking, cutting down on fat [in my diet], and changing.

I changed, first off, by dropping about forty pounds. Most people don't recognize me now. They ask, "Are you Salome Bey's daughter?"

There was a point in my life I used to diet, but this wasn't dieting. This was a way of life.

I asked friends of mine if they wanted to join me. Some did, some didn't. Those who didn't, I didn't make a fuss of.

I started walking, not because I didn't think I was beautiful; I knew I was. I had these old antique dresses I couldn't fit into. Either I had to throw them away, or find a way to put them on. Now I can put them on. And I don't think I'll ever go back to not being able to put them on again.

I must stress that what I have done is not dieting. This is a way of life. I eat everything, even more so than I did before, but the exercising has a way of taking care of it. For me to diet is to die. My husband is a chef. I still eat desserts. I have second helpings. And it feels good to know I can eat what I want.

I'm enjoying myself very much now. I'm not in a panic. I never think, "Oh my god, I've got to diet, or starve myself today." I never thought life could be like this. It feels very good.

Basically, I'm still big, bold and beautiful.

—Salome Bey, singer

The Balinese teenager who has his or her teeth filed, or an Ibibis girl who spends a year in a fattening house all give up their personal freedom and individuality for the sake of the society in which they live.

—Ted Polhemus, anthropologist/author

We don't have to be afraid of that little woman inside waiting to get out. We can get on with our lives. You can be just as stylish and look just as good when you're full-bodied. I certainly haven't put my life on hold.

—Margarietta St. Juste, Consul General, Jamaican Consulate General, Toronto

Not long ago, a television program sent out their news crew to follow me around Washington, D.C. At the time, there was a group of us protesting for rights, and such. The whole time, their reporter was somewhat hostile, and kept harassing me with the same tune: "You're a doctor; you know the health risks of being large. How can you advocate it? How can you be large?"

All I could say was: "You know, you're absolutely right. I am a doctor; I should know better. Explain to me why I am this size."

I would be remiss to say there are no health consequences. If there was a magic pill to save me from harassment and pain, I would take it. But there isn't one.

The physiological and emotional defense mechanisms are so inherent that trying to fight this thing, this natural tendency, is akin to trying to live without breathing. It's that tough. Millions of years ago when we were slimy creatures coming out of the oceans, we needed physiologic mechanisms to store energy, because we had to run and dig for our food. Now, millions of years later, the farthest we have to run is the local convenience store, the deepest we have to dig is in our pockets, but the hunger is still there. Most fat people are starving. It's that powerful a drive.

Imagine, if you will, how horrible life can be this way. They talk about how hard it is for the alcoholic, but you don't need alcohol to survive— you need food for survival. Staying away from it is insane. It's a physiological drive that can't be denied.

Add to it the fact that once your body's fat cells are enlarged they want to stay enlarged. Your body will lose everything else before [it loses fat], including muscle tissue. Which is why people die on starvation diets.

The prejudice is something else. In our society, we speak of the poor anorexic or the poor victim of bulimia; when have you ever heard about the poor fat victim? It's evil or vilified. You cannot say "Hey, babe," and be politically correct, but if you say "Hey, fatso," it's okay, it's humourous. Famous celebrities make endless ridicule of fat people and the crowd loves it.

Don't misunderstand me; I love comedy and goofy things. I don't mind humour or self-deprecating humour, but if they take all my ideas and don't give me credit, or treat me like dirt just because I'm fat— these are prejudice actions. These hurt and they're wrong. They're evil deeds.

In Fat Chance, *they showed us going to Virginia for a NAAFA meeting, but there was something they left out of the film. I talked for an hour and a half on what it's like to be fat. The whole audience was made up of dietitians and doctors who make a living trying to alter our bodies. You'd think they'd be angry at me talking heresy, but there wasn't a dry eye in the place. I was enlightened to see these health-care professionals being enlightened. I told them if they really cared about us, instead of trying to alter us and make us what we can never become, they would stop. We don't need their help, we need their support.*

I definitely believe there are health risks. Of course, I'd be remiss in saying otherwise, but we'll never be skinny, we'll never be thin. We have to realize what we are. And, mostly, we have to get on with life. We have to live.

—Dr. Moe Lerner, associate professor of emergency and family medicine, University of Manitoba; government health reform consultant; and star of the film *Fat Chance*

The bottom line is always the same–don't wait to live until you've finished dieting. You'll never be finished dieting. I dieted from the age of 16 to 28. Thank God, I didn't wait.

You can save yourself from victimhood by just living and looking your best. There are an awful lot of societal requirements of appearance–and they're all silly–but you can live fully however full you are. It's nuts not to. You're missing your life. You're living it according to someone else's rules, not your own. You know you're all right. We have absolutely no excuse for not taking our place in society. It's up to us to change things. And now we have all the raw materials at our fingertips to do so.

—Janey Milstead, Editor, *Big, Beautiful Women* magazine

Estimations of the old man's age at death range between 103 and 113, and that 108 must be taken as a conservative estimate . . . The portrait of this exceptional man suggests that he was stout, his bald head the shape of a rugby football, set on his body so that the ears would be near the pointed ends, and garnished with wisps of white hair. His mouth was small and puckered in mischief. That he was overweight is certain, but evidently he owed his unusual longevity to the fact that in those days there were no doctors competent to warn him of the dangers of obesity.

>—Peter Ustinov, actor/author, on his great-great-grandfather, Mikhail Adrianovitch

The reason I stuck with show business is because I have show business skills. I'm a dancer, a singer, an actress; I studied ballet, opera and acting. There's nothing in the theatre I can't do. I've got the life skills and the business skills, but I don't have any skills that would allow me to earn my living on a daily basis otherwise.

I know what I know, and I also know what I don't know.

And what keeps you going is sheer ignorance—a stupid, blind allegiance to something you love to do.

Those who wait for the day they'll be thin as the moment they'll be successful create a barrier for themselves, because they're afraid. What if they're skinny and they fail? If you fail as a person and you're fat, you have something to blame it on; and you'd be half right. But why not just be successful?

If you can't hide it, put a sequin on it. There's nothing worse than pretending something is there that isn't. Just sit down, eat yourself to death, enjoy yourself, and stop torturing yourself with dreams that will never be.

>—Liz Torres, actress

My philosophy of living large is the same philosophy no matter what size you are—stay true to yourself always.

Always listen to that sixth sense. Don't go against it. Feel good about who you are and how you are, and let your opinion of yourself always dominate.

It doesn't work trying to please everyone around you. It just doesn't. All these camouflages just get in the way. They get in the way of living and knowing, and trying to get closer to that sense of well-being and peace of mind, and everything you really need to make a good life for yourself.

It has nothing to do with the exterior ever. I learned this through hard knocks and being there. Being on the end of trying to please and trying to be what other people want you to be. I'm not there now, and I'm so comfortable with it. I might be a little sad walking away from someone who doesn't understand it, but it feels good knowing it's the right thing.

—Jackie Richardson, singer/actress

I believe that all women are goddesses, and goddesses come in all shapes and sizes. Just because a woman is plus-size doesn't mean she stops being sexy or living a full life.

—Delta Burke, actress

I didn't hear words at home like "fat" or "overweight." My mother always referred to me as "big," and I referred to me the same way. I am big. I'm 5'11", and I look good and feel best at about 190 pounds. Right now, I don't even know my size. I just try to look the very best I can at whatever size. I've dieted myself down to being rail thin. When I did DC Cab, *I was a size 11, but it's not my natural state. This is me, and I work out and exercise and try to turn some of me into muscle. I buy nice clothes, clothes that fit, and I don't want to be a size 4.*

If women did more talking to men as people, I think they'd be in for a few surprises. I rarely see a man running after a skinny woman. The woman who gets their attention has curves and boobs. Men like flesh. Have you ever seen a man go into a store and buy the skinniest steak he can find? You see men running behind women who have their heads held high.

There are big, attractive women, and there are some real ugly thin ones. Judge by size, and you'll miss out on a lot of good people and experiences.

—Marsha Warfield, comedian/actress

I wish society would quit putting all these external pressures on people. It's hard when every magazine you pick up sends the message that you have to be thin. Or when every store that you go into has clothes that only go up to a certain size, when almost every show you see on TV or in movies people are thin and beautiful. If you're happy, healthy and content with yourself, then people should just leave you the hell alone.

—Darlene Cates, actress

Fat people are sexy and attractive. Just like everybody else. It's okay to be fat. So you're fat. Just be fat and shut up about it.

—Roseanne, comedian/actress

In America right now, you will only see obese women among the working class. Fat has become déclassé. *Fat has become something to be ashamed of. You can't possibly rise in any corporation in America right now, if you're fat.*

I think many contemporary career women are ashamed of the fat woman. They're made very nervous by this fat woman, because she represents a kind of regression, back to the womb, a womb-like paralysis and so on, so they try to repress her.

Fat is too often seen as somehow a tool of the patriarchy that men are imposing on women. Low self-esteem that women looking at fashion magazines are being made to feel about themselves by some heterosexual conspiracy. Instead, I think women have to retake control of the imagery of fat.

I would like a return to a sense of the power of the fat woman, and not just that somehow she is a victim of her own body.

We've become too divorced from nature. We can see very clearly in something like Rubens, that the fat woman seems to be brimming over with vitality and energy. We see that she has some wonderful contact with nature. But, in the last twenty years of feminist discourse, nature's been wiped out.

—Camille Paglia, professor/author

Really, as far as I'm concerned, anorexia has replaced the corset. You used to be allowed to have a proper woman's body—a curvaceous body. You pull it in with a corset, you see a waist. I mean, why should we have to starve to be seen as beautiful? Marilyn [Monroe] was a size 16, you know? Isn't big beautiful, too?

If I was alive [in Rubens's time], I wouldn't have to be a comedian for a living. I would've been celebrated as a fabulous model, painted all day long.

In those days, model Kate Moss would only have had one use—as a paintbrush. I'd be there in Rubens's studio, he'd be painting me all the live-long day, and I'd say, "What's that in your hand, Rubens?"

He'd say, "It's Kate Moss. I'm using her as a paint brush."

—Dawn French, comedian/actress

ELEVEN

Still Fighting

I STILL DON'T HAVE it all down perfectly. And I probably won't. It's the great myth in my life, and it's something I've had to accept. I will never be perfect. In fact, I'm not sure what the word means. I'd actually like to eliminate the term from the dictionary. It's impossible to strive for something when you don't understand its definition. One's own perception of perfection may be entirely different from another's.

I don't even want to assume I'll be perfect. That was a high standard I put on myself for the longest time — something I was supposed to be striving for. It isn't possible for me, or anyone else, to be the perfect person. There's no such thing.

Nonetheless, I admit, I feel I have to be better. And this is part of my continuing battle.

I find I deprive myself of things, because I'm not better yet — almost as if I deny myself happiness, because I haven't reached some imaginary road mark.

There are still times when I don't allow myself to have certain foods, to treat myself or to go on a holiday—all the time thinking I haven't achieved what I want to achieve, or reached some elusive level of happiness to deserve what I consider luxuries.

There are times I find I settle for a lot less than I rightly deserve, rather than reaching for the best, knowing full well I have a right to the best of friends, the best restaurants, the best choice on the menu and the best of times. Deep down, we all want the best for ourselves; however, when you've spent years believing you don't measure up and you're not deserving, it takes some conditioning to conceive otherwise. Sometimes I still have to convince myself, and when I make a choice, I try to ensure I make the best one for me.

Basically, I have to loosen up. I have to free myself to reward myself for today. I need to free myself from the restraints and realize that if I pamper myself it's because I deserve it now. I need to focus on one day at a time, and realize I can give myself the luxury of enjoying who I am for today, instead of looking ahead and thinking I'll deserve it in another five years or however long it takes to achieve what needs to be achieved.

Don't misunderstand, I am happy. But now and then I get this feeling I don't merit happiness. Total and complete happiness. Every once in a while I have to remind myself I'm fine the way I am—that I am a wonderful, caring human being, who is beautiful from the inside out.

But, of course, there are still those occasional comments from the outside world, and although I have ways of dealing with them, I still have to deal with them.

And, this is one other continuing adjustment on my list of things to do. People continue to perceive me in a way that I do not see myself. And, when this happens it's almost as if they get in between me and the mirror—they get in the way.

I realize that until I rid myself of the significance others' opinions hold, I will not see myself clearly. And I want to be able to focus on myself. I want to look in the mirror and see a woman—nothing else. I want to go on believing size doesn't matter, that it isn't an issue.

Yet, I still wait for those negative comments. I stopped looking for them years ago, but I still have a here-we-go-again attitude. I still expect them.

And I'm still a little obsessed with my weight. There are times I have to point out to myself that the scales are not important. For years, the number on the dial made a difference to how I was going to handle the rest of my day or month. It controlled my moods. This preoccupation can have an effect on anyone, thin or large. It helped immensely to put away the scale; however, I never threw it away, and once in a blue moon, I take it out and blow off the dust.

After everything I've been through, I'm still hoping for the day that I don't think about it. That it will not only cease to be an issue, but it will actually be something I don't think about. It will just be.

None of these are new problems. They've been around for a while. We all have our old, knee-jerk reactions to familiar situations. There's no question my knees still jerk when I come up against my old demons.

Obviously, the biggest target in my battle is the continuing psychological effect of others' opinions. I desperately try not to be affected by their words. I know what I think is the only thing that matters, and being at peace with myself and happy with who I am is the only thing that counts. I also know when I find that peace, I'll find true happiness. I'll not only be able to hold happiness in my hand, I'll be able to hold it in my heart when I stop listening to them and listen to me.

It's not that I haven't been listening to myself, but when my voice is the only one I hear, that's when I'll know I've found peace; I've found my happiness. But I'm still moving to my old song-and-dance—two steps forward and one step back. This is just a step back.

One of the recurring themes in my life is the feeling that people need me and I can't disappoint them. I think I have to be a certain way, instead of realizing that if people need me, it doesn't matter what size I am, I can still be there for them. Instead of thinking I don't have to look a certain way or be a certain way to be useful, I focus on a fear of being rejected.

I have an innate fear of being rejected. Deep down inside, I worry that people will turn their backs on me, and it creates a need to be wanted. In the past, I found I would do anything to get the feeling that someone needed me, whether it was not saying anything while my ex-husband yelled about the number of calories on my dinner plate, or not speaking up when the modelling agency wanted me to gain or lose weight. I wanted to be needed, so I would adhere to anything. Even now, I have to remind myself that I am in the driver's seat, and no one else has control of the wheel.

I still tell myself that my body is merely a vehicle for my soul, and it's okay for my body to be a compact, mid-size or luxury model. It doesn't really matter what my body is. It's basically a vehicle that carries me through life. It comes down to where the soul is.

I admit this journey has been a confusing trip from day one. Throughout it all there have been quite a few bumps and I've been thrown off route a few times. But each time I've tried to get back on. Now, I honestly believe I'm on the right path. I'm on the route not only to good health but to a sound mind.

Before I can believe in anything else, I must believe in myself—the real me. I'm not looking for perfection, I'm looking for me. And until I find that—and I'm almost there—I can't speak of myself as if I am at that point. It wouldn't be honest.

I still travel through life being the best I can be, focusing on the wonderful person I am, and exuding energy on the things and people of importance in my world. My self-confidence, self-esteem and beauty are not measured by any scale. They're measured by my soul and my entire being.

And I suppose that's what I want. I want to be at peace. No doubt, I keep using the word "peace" because my life has been such a series of hills and valleys. I want a smooth ride now. I deserve it. I'm not naive enough to think I won't have more bumps along the way, and that they won't set me back, but at least if I'm settled with who I am and not striving or trying for something else, it will be much easier.

I just feel I've yet to be completely whole. I still look in the mirror and like what I see. I liked what I saw at size 24, at size 20 and at size 16. I've always liked myself. And that's the clincher right there. I never found anything wrong with me. It was the chatter all around me that played with my head, and made me feel that I wasn't good enough to meet others' standards. Their standards were always unimportant, but it was important enough to be accepted. So I catered to what was expected of me, but throughout it all, I looked in the mirror and liked what I saw. I liked who I was. But, as I've said, I didn't want to fight anymore, so I just became what they wanted. I became submissive. I thought it would be easier to do that than to fight for what I was.

However, for years now I've been saying, "No. I'm going to be what I am. Let my body take whatever course it takes to become a whole person." As long as I feel in my heart that I am a true, whole person, the rest doesn't matter. It doesn't matter what size I am, as long as I feel free within myself. That's what counts.

It counts, but it's still hard not to listen. The variables around me make it difficult sometimes to tune them out. I'm not a person who simply goes to a 9-to-5 job, where there aren't as many attitudes about appearance, where a person is not subjected every day to opinions about his or her body. Every single day of my life, people talk about my size. It's part of the job.

It's also part of my recreation. I go to a health club where I'm one of the biggest people. I know I am, and I know that people look at me from the corners of their eyes. It's okay; it doesn't matter, because I like who I am. This is one battle I've won. Take me back ten years and I would've crawled into the gym. I never would have let people look at me in judgement. It would have been devastating; I would have crawled right back out.

But, I spent years beating down the door of the small world — getting noticed, getting in, holding the door open for others, and making myself comfortable. And now I *am* comfortable.

I knew for years how the small world viewed the larger. Now, I find it quite astonishing how the larger world sees the small. Thin people are not the only ones who make comments because they have insecurities. It doesn't matter what size people are, what sex they are, or what colour they are; people will point at someone who's different if they're not happy with themselves.

I've always known this, but now I'm seeing it in a different light. Now—because of readjustments in eating habits and exercise—I'm fit and healthy. And now I'm perceived as thin in a large world. Large people come up to me and tell me I'm too small. This is another battle I've yet to overcome.

I've overcome being large in a small world. In a small world, I'm comfortable being large. It's the big world where I'm having some difficulty. I'm now uncomfortable in the large world, my world, my environment. To me, this is completely ironic. This is the true happiness I've yet to find. This is the peace I still have to make.

For years I was on one side of the fence, fighting for equality; now I seem to have been thrown to the other side. And once again I see how horribly unfair it is for there to be any discrimination regarding size. This is a very personal dilemma for me.

In a sense, I feel I'm being somewhat rejected for who I am now, even with the appreciation of what I have been and what I've done. This adds insult to injury. I have been there, and my peers are all aware I was a very big woman for a very long time, one who strongly supported them and their beliefs, and carved a few paths and opened a few doors, and continues to do so. This perception of me, this new found perception of me, is merely a perception of body size. Which proves many minds can be so shallow and many memories so short-lived.

Once more, I'm being appraised from the outside. There are people who are not getting past my exterior, not seeing the inside. It's happening all over again.

These people who only see me from an exterior standpoint seem to think I no longer understand because I'm no longer a size 24. I find myself telling them, "I understand. I don't have to be there physically to understand. I *was* there. I *am* there. I'll always be there." I explain to them that I've become a diabetic and have had no choice but to alter my habits in order to live longer, which in effect, I should never have to explain. I'm still a plus-size person. I'm still the person I've always been inside and I still believe, and these things will never change.

I've had too many things happen in my life and fought too many battles not to believe what I'm saying. I've been through it all, how could I not believe? The fact that their perceptions of me are based merely on my size, the way I look and the tag at the back of my blouse astonishes me, disappoints me and makes me think my entire battle for size acceptance has not been heard. They may have watched my lips moving, but they didn't listen. They never got the point.

The point, and what everything boils down to, is that size is not an issue. It's about equality. It's about the whole person. It doesn't matter if a person is fat, thin, tall, short, black, white, young, old, male, female—that person is an individual. How long will it take for all of us to understand this? How long will it take for all of us to get the point?

One of my saddest moments happened recently, when a lovely young woman approached the register in the boutique. She put some clothing on the counter, looked at me and asked, "How does it feel to be smaller than you used to be, Jackqueline?"

"What do you mean, how does it feel?" I asked.

She told me she was a size 20 and wasn't happy about it.

"You're a beautiful woman," I said. "How does it feel to be a beautiful woman?"

"I'm not beautiful," she answered. "God gave me a beautiful body, but I've abused it, and I deserve to be punished for the way I've treated it."

When I hear comments like these, it floors me. I feel like I'm starting all over again. It makes you realize that no matter how many times you say the words, there will still be people out there who haven't been affected by their meaning. There's still so much teaching and preaching to be done. There are still so many people who need to be touched.

In a way, I saw myself in her eyes. And, in a way, I saw myself back at the beginning. I looked at her and saw a beautiful woman; she saw herself as someone who deserved to be punished. It's times like these that remind me I still have a fight on my hands. As they say, I may have won the battle, but I haven't won the war.

I'm still fighting the war, and it's been one arduous battle after another. There are times I feel like a lonely soldier up against a distant troop. And, many times the soldiers are just like me (sometimes our worst enemy is ourselves). But whether I stand alone or alongside my allies, there are still victories left to win. When that young woman made that comment, a whole battlefield opened up again, and I prepared myself for war.

I found myself swinging around and telling her how beautiful she was, and making sure she left the boutique with her head high. She came back not long after. She made a bee-line for me with a smile on her face, a smile full of gratitude. It made me feel good to know that I had touched her, that she felt good about herself, even if it had been for a brief moment. If that happened, it was worth the battle.

These are the moments that remind me I need to strengthen my resources and call in for reinforcements. I need to bolster that inner strength, and I need to be a whole person. I need to be that whole person so I can reach out to people and, possibly, touch them. Because when I do, I think maybe, just maybe, I can win the war. It's the inner peace that makes it possible to go on fighting.

I remind myself that every negative experience I encounter has a positive outcome. And this gives me reason to believe circumstances can only get better. Believing every negative situation has a lesson makes me a stronger person. When you learn from a challenge, it becomes a positive situation.

I've never looked at my life and wished it had been different. When I look at my life, it seems like it's been set up to be this way, as one continuous learning curve. Travelling this path, I can look back and see every moment that seemed dark and bleak was simply that—a moment. I've looked at situations and wondered how I could improve them, how I could avoid them or how I could help someone else avoid them. And, looking for a solution, focusing on the positive, also leaves no time to dwell on the negative or unnecessary. When life is like this—when every day holds its own lesson—the long journey can't help but be an enlightening, uplifting experience.

The Beginning

APPENDIX

Supporting Ideas

THE NOTION THAT PEOPLE should be accepted by society, as well as themselves, regardless of size is moving around the globe—from the Women at Large organization in Hawthorndene, South Australia, to the Overweight Society in Stockholm, Sweden. Here are some objective and universal thinkers closer to home.

Ample Opportunity (AO)

Based in Portland, Oregon, this group embraces the idea that larger women can be happy and healthy now. They offer a monthly newsletter, monthly meeting and activities such as swimming, tai chi, canoeing and belly dancing. Write AO, P.O. Box 40621, Portland, OR 97240, U.S.A., or phone (503) 245-1524.

Body Image Task Force

"Dedicated to promoting the concept of positive body-image for all people," is this group's motto. Fighting "looksism" at every corner—be that discrimination against height, weight or physical characteristics—they offer community presentations, a newsletter and various brochures. The Body Image Task Force can be reached at P.O. Box 934, Santa Cruz, CA 95061-0934, U.S.A. (they ask that you send along stamps, envelopes are not necessary), or phone (408) 457-4838.

Body-Pride

As their name implies, these folks are "dedicated to providing education and awareness on eating disorders, weight preoccupation, body image and self-esteem." They aim to "encourage women of all ages to dispel society's unrealistic beauty ideal and to indulge in a splendour of accepting, respecting and loving the natural bodies they have been given." Body-Pride conducts lectures and workshops at a variety of locations and organizations, including schools and women's centres, and also publishes a magazine of the same name. For information write to Body-Pride, 7B Pleasant Boulevard, Suite 1015, Toronto, Ont., M4T 1K2, Canada, or phone (416) 486-3710.

Diet Breakers

Working with government and the medical profession to regulate the diet industry, this British size-acceptance organization titles its program, "You count, calories don't." They are also responsible for creating the annual May 6 International No Diet Day. For information, send a self-addressed, postage-paid envelope to Diet Breakers, Barford St. Michael, Banbury, Oxon OX15 OUA, England.

Diet/Weight Liberation
This group, affiliated with New York's Cornell University, goes by the slogan, "We advocate a non-dieting, size-accepting approach to health, fitness and self-esteem." Apart from being involved in various size-acceptance programs, including a ten-session psycho-educational support group called Full-Bodied and Fabulous, they hold celebrations and activities for Size-Acceptance Month in October and No-Diet Day in May. Write to Terry Nicholetti Garrison, Director, Diet/Weight Liberation, CRESP, Anabel Taylor Hall, Cornell University, Ithaca, NY 14853, U.S.A., or phone (607) 257-0563.

Largesse
The international resource network for body-esteem offers both support and information. Its computer database is packed with resources and ideas. To find out more, send a self-addressed, postage-paid envelope to Largesse, P.O. Box 9404, New Haven, CT 06534-0404, U.S.A., or phone/fax (203) 787-1624.

NAAFA (National Association to Advance Fat Acceptance)
NAAFA's goal is to stop size-discrimination and offer the tools necessary to build self-fulfillment. This North American non-profit human rights organization works as an advocate and educator, and offers its members both information and support mechanisms, including a bi-monthly newsletter and introductory workbook on size awareness. For more information write NAAFA, P.O. Box 188620, Sacramento, CA 95818 U.S.A., or phone (916) 558-6880 or, toll-free, 1 (800) 442-1214.

National Eating Disorder Information Centre, The
A program of the Toronto Hospital, this information centre offers a slew of data to women all across Canada. Equipped with a national resource directory, NEDIC is able to furnish anyone with information on food and weight preoccupation, and also refer you to an organization or program close to home. Their motto is "celebrating our natural sizes"; their address is 200 Elizabeth St., C1-211, Toronto, Ont., M5G 2C4, Canada, or phone (416) 340-4156.

People at Large (PAL)
Based in Toronto, this non-profit group offers a social, information and support network of large people in the Toronto and surrounding areas. PAL's motto is "united to promote size acceptance, self-esteem, and social integration"; it can be reached at PAL, P.O. Box 11522, 600 The East Mall, Etobicoke, Ont., M9B 4B0, Canada.

Sheena's Place
In honour of Sheena Carpenter (a young woman who died grappling with the effects of anorexia), this non-profit organization was set up to aid those dealing with eating disorders and body image concerns. It offers help in five areas—peer and group support; personal growth; vocational counselling; relaxation and stress management therapies; and information education— for individuals as well as family members and caregivers. For more information, write Sheena's Place, 333 King St. E., Toronto, Ont., M5A 3X5, Canada, or phone (416) 947-2365.

Women and Body Image Project

This project, created and run by the Regional Women's Health Centre at Toronto's Women's College Hospital, provides support, education, counseling, advocacy and consultation for a full range of body image concerns. The program offers aid on an individual basis to adult women; holds summer retreats, called Embodying Equity, for youth; and also provides counseling models to other health professionals. For further information, call Carla Rice at (416) 351-3704, or write Women and Body Image Project at the Regional Women's Health Centre, 790 Bay St., 8th floor, Toronto, Ont., M5G 1N9, Canada.

Women's Health Clinic

Apart from a variety of health services, the medical professionals at the Women's Health Clinic in Winnipeg, Manitoba, also give lessons on self-esteem and body acceptance. Getting Beyond Weight is a two-hour information session that addresses weight issues. It's held once a month, and is free to any interested party. The Clinic's Weight Preoccupation Support Group, again available to anyone, is a more extensive ten-week program. Information packages are available for both programs. For more information, phone the clinic at (204) 947-1517.

YOU*NIQUE

Here, Kaca Henley says, "we talk about the uniqueness of each individual, and the worthiness of every individual," within the group's self-esteem strategy seminars.

"I don't claim to have the answer. I maintain we each have our own answers. We deal with ways to bolster the constructive ones, and defuse the unconstructive ones, and find ways to help each other pull ourselves up."

YOU*NIQUE welcomes all women, regardless of size, shape or age, and offers personalized audiotapes to strengthen self-interest. For a brochure or more information, write the organization at 620 Jarvis St., Suite 1023, Toronto, Ont., M4Y 2R8, Canada, or call Kaca (Kach-a) Henley at (416) 964-0292, toll-free 1 (800) 663-9102. Or e-mail at khenley@interlog.com.

Bibliography

Brett, Anwar. "Depp's Prom Queen." *Yes!*, September 1995, p. 35.

Brown, Catrina and Jasper, Karin. *Consuming Passions: Feminist Approaches to Weight Preoccupation and Eating Disorders*. Toronto: Second Story Press, 1993.

Canadian Dietetic Association, The. "Association Position." *Journal of The Canadian Dietetic Association*, Spring 1995, 138.

Fishman, Laurel. "Big Beautiful Women of the '90s: Plus-Size Stars in the Entertainment Firmament." *Big Beautiful Woman BBW*, Winter 1995, p. 38.

French, Dawn. *Dawn French on Big Women*, one-hour television special. London: LWT, 1994.

Health Services and Promotional Branch, Health and Welfare Canada. *Promoting Healthy Weights: A Discussion Paper*. October 1988.

Marchessault, Gail D.M. "Weight Preoccupation in North American Culture." *Journal of The Canadian Dietetic Association*, Fall 1993, p. 138.

McDonald, Paul. W. "A Case for the Treatment of Obesity." *Journal of The Canadian Dietetic Association*, Fall 1995, p. 131.

Milstead, Janey. "TV's Number One BBW." *Big Beautiful Woman BBW*, August 1989.

Milstead, Janey. "Marsha Warfield." *Big Beautiful Woman BBW*, September 1989, p. 28.

Polhemus, Ted. *Body Styles*. London: Lennard Books Ltd., 1988.

Polhemus, Ted and the Institute of Contemporary Arts. *The Body Reader: Social Aspects of the Human Body*. London: Penguin Books Ltd., 1978.

Schnurnberger, Lynn. *Let There Be Clothes: A Fashion Timeline*. New York: Workman Publishing, 1991.

The Body Shop. *The Body Shop Book: Skin, Hair and Body Care*. London: Little, Brown and Company, 1994.

Ustinov, Peter. *Dear Me*. Boston, Toronto: Atlantic-Little, Brown Books, 1977.

What's been said about Jackqueline Hope:

"Jackqueline Hope didn't call her business Big, Bold & Beautiful for nothing. It's a philosophy she follows to the last letter. She's a big woman, she's beautiful and she believes in bold speaking, bold living and bold dressing."
— Valerie Gibson, Fashion Editor, *The Toronto Sun*

"Jackqueline Hope has earned her name as president of Big, Bold & Beautiful. She offers a sense of confidence and optimism to a slew of North American women."
— *The Globe and Mail*

"Major designers are jumping into the plus size market, but no one knows the market better than Jackqueline Hope, president of Big, Bold & Beautiful."
— *You Magazine*

"As president of Big, Bold & Beautiful/Plus Figure Models, [Jackqueline] champions accentuating the positive."
— *Canadian Living* magazine

"Jackqueline Hope, impeccably dressed, polished and confident, weighs more than 200 lbs; and she couldn't care less. She used to care, but she's over that now. Hope...is now spending her days persuading other women not to care either."
— *The Toronto Star*

"Women on the Move nominee Jackqueline Hope loves telling large-size women how much they can have. As far as Hope's concerned, they can have it all. They can have everything from a successful career to a great love life. Hope has parlayed her own career as a large-size model into big business."
— David Graham, *The Toronto Sun*

"Jackqueline Hope is a whirlwind. She talks nonstop, she works nonstop and she has an energy level that would put the Energizer Bunny to shame. She loves her life."

—*Big, Beautiful Woman* magazine

"There is a cheerleader for larger women, large people. Her name is Jackqueline Hope…"

—Marilyn Dennis, Cityline

"Jackqueline Hope has been designing the Big, Bold & Beautiful line and outfitting plus-size celebrities and models for more than a decade. Over the years, she has become an expert on plus-size fashions and not only does she incorporate current trends into her collection, she also sets the trends."

—Alicia Kay, CFTO News

"Society has changed and Jackqueline is at the forefront of this change. [She] is changing peoples' lives."

—Dini Petty, host of Dini

"We're backstage at a fashion show here in Toronto, but this isn't any ordinary fashion show, this is a show that only caters to larger women. The show's organizer and guiding light is Jackqueline Hope. Hope became a plus-size activist and entrepreneur through first-hand experience."

—Fashion Television's Jeanne Beker at the
Big, Bold & Beautiful fashion show

"Jackqueline Hope has always been ahead of her time. Not only was she Canada's first plus-size model, but she parlayed that career into a burgeoning plus-size fashion business back in the early 1980s."

— Connie Smith, News at Noon

To receive more information about the
Big, Bold & Beautiful catalogue or Big On Fitness,
phone 416-923-4673
or toll free 1-800-668-4673; fax 416-923-5673;
or write to:

Big, Bold & Beautiful
1263 Bay Street
Toronto, Ontario
M5R 2C1, Canada

About the Author

Jackqueline Hope is a staunch supporter of size acceptance. She has held fast to the belief that life is measured by more than just a dress size, and has made it her life's work to prove it.

Canada's first plus-size model, Jackqueline parlayed her knowledge of beauty and fashion into Big, Bold & Beautiful, Inc., a company she founded at the age of 25.

Since 1981, the business has grown to include the country's largest plus-size modelling agency, Plus-Figure Models, as well as its leading clothing boutiques, Big, Bold & Beautiful and Big, Bold & Beautiful Brides.

Apart from presiding over the business as president and CEO, Jackqueline is also a fashion designer, creating the company's exclusive plus-size label, Jackie Jackie, which spans an entire wardrobe from casualwear to eveningwear.

To serve those unable to visit the boutique, she launched the Big, Bold & Beautiful mail-order catalogue in 1992. Published four times a year, the shop-at-home service is now used by more than 55,000 women in North America, Europe, Asia, Britain and Australia.

More recently, Jackqueline has added health advocate to her role. As co-founder of Big On Fitness, she offers a step-by-step exercise program that encourages a healthy attitude toward physical activity and guides plus-size women along the road to overall well-being.

Sought after for her refreshing attitude and business philosophy, she has been featured on FashionTelevision, VH1 House of Style, CityLine, Eye on Toronto, CFTO's By Design, Dini, BreakfastTelevision, and also covered by countless newspapers, magazines and radio talk shows.